WARBIRD**TECH**
SERIES

VOLUME 42

SUKHOI
Su-27 FLANKER

YEFIM GORDON AND PETER DAVISON

specialtypress
PUBLISHERS AND WHOLESALERS

Published by
Specialty Press Publishers and Wholesalers
39966 Grand Avenue
North Branch, MN 55056
United States of America
(800) 895-4585 or (651) 277-1400
http://www.specialtypress.com

Distributed in the UK and Europe by
Midland Publishing
4 Watling Drive
Hinckley LE10 3EY, England
Tel: 01455 254 450 Fax: 01455 233 737
http://www.midlandcountiessuperstore.com

ISBN-13 978-1-58007-091-1
ISBN-10 1-58007-091-4

Material contained in this book is intended for historical and entertainment value only, and is not to be construed as usable for aircraft or component restoration, maintenance, or use.

Printed in China

Front Cover:
Main: The Su-30MKK features taller, increased-area CFRP fins with integral tanks a la Su-35. Note the "brandy stripes" on the fins of this one and just how far forward of the stabilators lie the twin fins. (Sukhoi OKB)

Inset: A top view of the T10K-7 with a standard complement of AAMs. (Military Technology)

Back Cover:
Top Right: The T10V-5's rather yucky "greenbottle fly" camouflage is effective for over-water sorties. (Yefim Gordon)

Middle: A spectacular view of two of eight Su-27Ks (Su-33s) flown to Kubinka for the 50th anniversary of the victory in the Great Patriotic War in April 1995. The flying control positions for an afterburner take-off can be seen clearly. (Yefim Gordon)

Bottom: The cockpit interior of a single-seat Su-27. The red lever to the right jettisons the canopy. The magnetic compass is fixed to the canopy frame beside the HUD. (Sukhoi OKB archive)

Title Page:
The Su-34 (Air Force designation Su-27IB) had its debut in 2000, taking part in a Russian Air Force exercise. (Sukhoi OKB)

TABLE OF CONTENTS

SUKHOI SU-27 FLANKER

ACKNOWLEDGMENTS

The authors wish to thank the translator of this book, Dmitriy Komissarov; this book would never have been accomplished without him, and he also made several useful additions to the text. Also, the authors wish to thank the following persons for their contributions:

Andrey Yurgenson for making numerous line drawings for this book; Valentin Vetlitskiy for his color artwork; Vladimir Antonov and Vladimir Yakovlev at the Sukhoi OKB; Viltor Drooshlyakov and Pavel Maslov for their excellent photos taken aboard the aircraft carrier; Andrey Fomin for supplying valuable information on systems development.

INTRODUCTION

Known to many as "Flanker," the Su-27 single-seat supersonic interceptor is a fourth-generation Soviet fighter and has come to be generally recognized as one of the world's best fighters of the 1990s. It was a joint product of the design bureau (OKB—*opytno-konstrooktorskoye byuro*) led by Pavel Osipovich Sukhoi, the engine design bureau led by Arkhip Mikhaylovich Lyul'ka, the State Research Institute of Aircraft Systems (GosNII AS—*Gosoodahrstvennyy naoochno-issledovatel'skiy institoot aviatseeonnykh sistem*)—and many other research, engineering, and industrial organizations—thereby employing the latest know-how gained by the Soviet aerospace industry.

Excellent performance, handling, and serviceability have made the aircraft popular with its pilots and ground personnel alike. The aircraft has become the progenitor of a whole family of high-performance combat jets, one of which, the Su-27K (Su-33), is the first Soviet aircraft to make a conventional landing on an aircraft carrier.

To answer the inevitable question of the Flanker's origins, it must be stated that two main factors were responsible for the Su-27's appearance. The internal factor, so to say, was the Sukhoi OKB's long-standing tradition as a fighter maker. In the postwar years the company produced three successful interceptors: the Su-9 Fishpot-A/B, the Su-11 Fishpot-C, and the Su-15 Flagon.

The other major factor was the U.S. aerospace industry that had by then produced the Grumman F-14 Tomcat, an excellent shipboard fighter, and was in the middle of a dedicated heavy fighter program. McDonnell Douglas eventually won the contract for the F-15 Eagle. Echoes of that program were naturally heard in the USSR via intelligence channels, and Sukhoi was thinking of a suitable answer.

Lessons learned with third-generation tactical aircraft—the Su-15, Su-17, Su-24, MiG-23, MiG-25, F-5E, F-4, F-111, and Mirage F1—showed that the follow-on should be a dedicated fighter and every effort should be directed at enhancing its counter-air capability. Therefore, it seems quite natural that in late 1969 a small group of engineers in Sukhoi's preliminary design (PD) section would start working on such a fighter—the fighter that was to gain worldwide fame in its definitive shape: The Su-27.

CONCEPT & EARLY DEVELOPMENT

A model of an early version of the T-10 project. (Sukhoi OKB archive)

In 1971, research institutes of the Ministry of Aircraft Industry (MAP—*Ministerstvo aviatseeonnoy promyshlennosti*) and the VVS began developing fighter force re-equipment concepts for the '80s.

Ideally the Air Force should have several kinds of fighters with weapons systems optimized for various mission types. An interceptor needs a good rate of climb, heavy armament, and capable avionics. An escort fighter should have sufficient range, high maneuverability, a high thrust-to-weight ratio, and a wide speed range. A possible solution was to build an advanced tactical fighter (ATF) and an advanced mass-produced light fighter (AMLF)[1] optimized for operations over friendly territory.

The ATF would have a sizeable internal fuel and ordnance load (at least four medium-range air-to-air missiles in addition to short-range or "dogfight AAMs" and a built-in gun) and a comprehensive navigation, communications, and electronic support measures (ESM) suite. With a specially configured avionics and weapons fit, it could be operated by the PVO's fighter arm (IA PVO—*istrebeetel'naya aviatsiya PVO*).

The ATF and AMLF would account for 30 to 35% and 65 to 70% of the fighter force, respectively, being the Soviet answer to the F-16 and the F-15. This concept was the brainchild of TsNII-30 (*Tsentrahl'nyy naoochno-issledovatel'skiy institoot*—Central R&D Institute No. 30), a division of the Ministry of Defense.

The Sukhoi OKB took on the ATF part of the re-equipment program with first sketches completed in February 1970. The aircraft had an integral layout with the wings and fuselage blended into a single lifting body, twin tails, and low-mounted stabilizers. The engines were housed in spaced underslung nacelles. The fighter had a large bubble canopy offering an excellent 360° view, aided by a downward-angled forward fuselage.

The ATF project received the in-house code T-10; the blended wing/body Version A and the more conventional Version B were known initially as T10-1 and T10-2, respectively (not to be confused with manufacturer's designations of the actual prototypes). Pavel O. Sukhoi let the leaders of TsAGI (*Tsentrahl'nyy aero- i gidrodinameecheskiy institoot*—Central Aerodynamics and Hydrodynamics Institute, named after Nikolay V. Zhukovskiy) examine the project and won their support. Wind-tunnel models of both versions were made and tested. The verdict was clear: the integral layout was better, mainly because of the lower drag in supersonic cruise, and so the angular T10-2 was discontinued.

The layout had some completely new design features. The spaced engine nacelles were attached to the wing undersurface with the upper intake lip acting as a boundary layer splitter plate. The center of gravity (CG) was located well aft, making the aircraft statically unstable in the pitch channel and thus enhancing maneuverability. The T-10 was the first Soviet aircraft to feature, in planned production form, an automated fly-by-wire (FBW) control system with no direct mechanical link between the stick and pedals and the control surfaces. These features contributed to the success of the definitive Su-27 and the whole Flanker family.

In 1971 the Soviet MoD issued a request for proposals concerning next-generation fighters. Three famous fighter design bureaus led by P. O. Sukhoi, Artyom Ivanovich Mikoyan, and Aleksandr Sergeyevich Yakovlev joined the race. Mikoyan submitted two versions of the MiG-29 Fulcrum; Yakovlev entered the Yak-45M light fighter and the Yak-47 heavy fighter, while Sukhoi's entries were the T10-1 and T10-2.

The real contest began in 1972 when the VVS examined the projects. Sukhoi representatives were armed with the results of TsAGI wind-tunnel tests and calculations and managed to create a sufficiently good impression. The project commission recommended the T10-1 and the MiG-29 to fill the heavy ATF and LTF requirements, respectively. The full-scale development stage began next. The T-10 was the first statically unstable aircraft with FBW controls designed in the Soviet Union.

Several high-ranking OKB officials (deputy chief project engineer I. Baslavskiy, PD section chief M. Khesin,

A model of another version of the T-10. All versions had ogival wings at the advanced project stage. (Yefim Gordon)

and design team leader L. Chernov) made a major contribution to the T-10 program by researching the aerodynamics of ogival (S-shaped) wings. The T-10's wings, optimized for transonic and supersonic flight, featured prominent LERXes (Leading Edge Root Extensions) integrated into the fuselage. The big question was whether they would assist with the required high maneuverability.

To answer this question, the OKB addressed SibNIA (*Seebeerskiy naoochno-issledovatel'skiy institoot aviatsii*), the Siberian Aviation Research Institute in Novosibirsk. SibNIA's involvement in the T-10 program lasted 12 years.

The first batch of "Siberian" models built in 1973 consisted of two

separate ogival wing sections. One model had a flat upper surface, while the other had the original version of the optimum upper surface curvature at the root. The models were tested in the T-203 low-speed wind tunnel at angles of attack (AOAs) between 0° and 40°. After testing on dynamometric scales and tests with different airflow visualization methods (using wool tufts, chord-wise and span-wise grids, and oil film), SibNIA engineers filmed on the characteristics of the ogival wing during maneuvers and measured airflow aft of the wing. Later, pressure sensors were built into the models to examine pressure distribution over the wing surface. Thus, comprehensive data was obtained experimentally over the first two years.

SibNIA engineers immediately started modifying the wings to find ways of improving performance. The sculpted upper surface of model No. 2 ensured smooth airflow in subsonic cruise even on the complex ogival wing. At moderate alpha (6 to 8°), the LERXes generated powerful vortices and a second pair of vortices appeared on the outer wing leading edges. They increased lift, improving lift/drag ratio, and were ideal for high maneuverability. However, as the AOA increased past 10°, the vortices grew and merged. The effect was similar to a tip stall spreading inboard over a large area—with all its negative consequences: Pitch-up, deterioration of lift and lateral stability, and pulsating aerodynamic loads.

A major improvement was clearly needed. SibNIA was facing two tasks: (1) finding the correct shape of the LERXes so as to intensify and maintain the vortices at AOAs at which the aircraft normally maneuvers; and (2) intensifying and maintaining the vortices generated by the outer wing LE (leading edge) so as to prevent premature merging of the two vortices. Apart from low-speed wind-tunnel tests, SibNIA also tested the T-10's wings in its T-205M transonic wind tunnel and in the ITPM's[2] T-313 supersonic wind tunnel leased for the occasion.

By the mid '70s, however, the OKB's interest in aerodynamic research at SibNIA waned. Pavel O. Sukhoi appointed his venerable and respected deputy, Yevgeniy A. Ivanov, as project chief. Work on the T-10 in Moscow and Novosibirsk seemed to progress in two different worlds. A group of Sukhoi employees received a patent for the initial configuration of the fighter. Tests with a model representing a complete aircraft began in 1975 and revealed poor control efficiency, roll, and yaw stability.

WARBIRDTECH
SERIES

A full-scale mockup of the T-10 as presented to the State Mockup Inspection Commission. (Sukhoi OKB archive)

As a point of interest, SibNIA also worked on a forward-swept wing (FSW) version of the Su-27. The results of this research later proved invaluable to Sukhoi in designing the S-37 Berkut (Golden Eagle) FSW technology demonstrator—which, incidentally, has a substantial degree of structural commonality with the Su-27 and its versions.

A major shortcoming of the T10-1 was its landing gear design. The nose unit was fairly straightforward, though the complex curvature of the lower forward fuselage gave trouble. The main gear units originally retracted between the engine nacelles. The retraction sequence was complex and the wheel track was narrow, creating taxiing problems. Additionally, the main-wheel wells cut into several fuselage main-

frames at the wing/fuselage joint where the aerodynamic loads were greatest. Placing the main wheels in the center fuselage increased the fighter's maximum cross-section and associated drag.

The under-slung engines with low-mounted intakes proved vulnerable to foreign object damage (FOD). To provide adequate ground clearance, the landing gear had to be longer and heavier than on fighters with conventional fuselages. A revised version of the project, designated T10-3, featured main gear units retracting into the bottoms of the engine nacelles as in the F-15. The T10-3 also incorporated aerodynamic changes based on the wind-tunnel tests of the T10-1.

The next version, T10-5, appeared in 1973. This differed from earlier configurations in having the engine

accessory gearboxes located dorsally, decreasing the maximum cross-section area. The T10-6A, developed late in the same year, introduced major changes. Like the T10-5, it was an integral-layout aircraft with engines in spaced nacelles, a bubble canopy, twin tails, and low-mounted stabilators. However, it featured axi-symmetric air intakes that decreased nacelle length and overall surface area and drag. For the first time the main gear units retracted into fairings outboard of the engine nacelles so that the wheels lay horizontally in the wing roots.

The T10-6 was likewise a blended wing/body design, but the engines were located in a common nacelle with a single air intake divided by a vertical wedge into port and starboard halves; three-segment vertical intake ramps were attached to the wedge, however, wind tunnel tests gave disappointing results and the T10-6 was abandoned.

By late 1974 the T-10's general arrangement and structural and aerodynamic concepts had crystallized. The design was finally frozen in 1975 and a set of documents issued for the construction of the first prototype.

Engine Development

Several Soviet engine design bureaus started working on appropriate engines in the late 1960s. In the mid-70s, Arkhip M. Lyul'ka finally implemented his invention—the turbofan engine.[3] His first afterburning turbofan, the AL-31F, was rated at 7,600 kgp (16,755 lb st) dry and 12,500 kgp (27,557 lb st) reheat. It was a spinoff of the AL-21F-3 afterburning turbojet.

The AL-31F was Lyul'ka's greatest achievement. It had a modular design, a shorter-than-average afterburner chamber, and a convergent-divergent supersonic nozzle. Unusually, the accessories gearbox was a separate unit

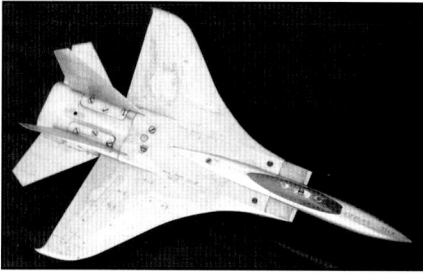
A metal wind-tunnel model of an early T10 version; note the option to change or adjust the fin profiles

located ahead of the engine and driven by a long extension shaft. Besides the usual engine accessories, it had a jet fuel starter (called turbostarter in Russian), which is an auxiliary power unit (APU) that kept the hydraulic and electric systems operational in the event of engine failure. The AL-31F featured a full-authority analog engine control system and a backup hydro-mechanical control system. The engine was to run smoothly at all operational AOAs.

Systems Development

In 1973, when the ATF/LTF contest was over, TsNII-30 completed another survey of the Soviet Air Force's fighter requirements, this time with specific aircraft in mind (the T-10 and MiG-29). The institute issued revised specific operational requirements (SORs) for the two types in the same year. The most stringent demands were applied to the avionics. The fire-control radar was to work in multiple wavebands and be capable of detecting and tracking multiple targets. The avionics were to be based on semiconductors instead of the vacuum tubes used hitherto, be lighter, more compact, and more reliable. The aircraft were to be equipped with an optoelectronic targeting system comprising an infrared search and track (IRST) unit and a laser rangefinder. Also required were a head-up display (HUD) and a cathode-ray tube (CRT) indicator.

In the T-10 and MiG-29, the first Soviet fighters with digital avionics, the extremely stringent operational requirements (high speed and multiple functions) meant the designers faced quite a few problems. As a result, NPO "Elektroavtomatika" developed the TsVM-800 computer for the T-10. GosNII AS contributed much to designing and refining the T-10's avionics suite. A lab was specially organized at GosNII AS for debugging avionics software. The institute and Sukhoi OKB jointly built a special simulation complex. It was used for testing the fire-control radar, optoelectronic targeting system, and weapons control system.

Weaponry

Another major development program concentrated on weapons. Originally, both the ATF and the LTF were to be armed with a 23-mm Gryazev/Shipunov GSh-23 (AO-9) or 30-mm GSh-30 (AO-17) twin-barrel fast-firing automatic gun, K-27[4] advanced medium-range AAMs, and K-14 or K-73 short-range AAMs. The ATF had four medium-range AAMs and four or six short-range AAMs while the LTF had two and four, respectively.

At the same time there was a contest going on between the missile makers. The "Vympel" (Pennant) and "Molniya" (Lightning) bureaus were vying for the K-27 medium-range AAM. Vympel's entry, developed by chief project engineer A. L. Lyapin, came out as the winner.

Unlike all AAMs existing in the Soviet Union or elsewhere, the K-27 had an inertial guidance mode. The target was initially illuminated by the fighter's radar, and the missile switched to its own radar at the terminal guidance phase. This considerably increased effective kill range, allowing the pilot to fire his missiles before the "bad guy"

did so, and it was expected to give Soviet fighters a considerable advantage over the F-15 and McDonnell Douglas F/A-18 Hornet armed with Sparrows. After entering production in 1984–87, the missile was re-designated R-27 (for *raketa*) and received the NATO code name AA-10 Alamo.

The same companies (Vympel and Molniya) were working on short-range (12-20 km/6-11 nm) AAMs, or "dogfight missiles." Vympel developed the K-14 – a thorough update of the K-13M (AA-2 Atoll) and K-13M1 (AA-2-2 Advanced Atoll) with an omni-directional IR tracker head and higher G limits. Molniya designed the all-new K-73 wingless missile with a jet control system and an IR tracker head with a limited field of view. In 1983 NPO Molniya switched to ballistic missiles; the aircraft group was transferred to ex-rival Vympel OKB – which got all the credit when the missile entered production two years later as the R-73/AA-11 Archer.

In the mid-70s GosNII AS's Sections 3 and 4 began a unique research and development program called "Zarya" (dawn; pronounced *zaryah*) at the request of the VVS. The subject of this program was enhanced rear hemisphere protection of fighters by means of firing AAMs backwards! The main complication of this innovative approach was that the missile inevitably experiences zero velocity as it parts company with the aircraft and hence becomes unstable and uncontrollable, since conventional rudders no longer work. A possible solution was to use jet control, just as on the R-73. Later, the appearance of a rear-hemisphere radar, which would detect pursuing enemy fighters and guide missiles to them, strengthened the feasibility of the idea.

Thus, by the mid 70s the USSR had research programs going in every aspect of fourth-generation fighter design – aerodynamics, propulsion, avionics, armament, you name it.

IMPROVEMENTS

T10-1, the first prototype, in the assembly shop of Sukhoi's experimental plant. (Sukhoi OKB archive)

T10-1 and T10-2 Interceptor Prototypes

In 1975 the Sukhoi OKB started issuing working drawings for the construction of the first prototype Su-27, designated T10-1. Even as prototype construction commenced, it became clear that the original aerodynamic layout had problems. Still, T10-1 was duly completed; the OKB leaders wanted to test the aircraft in "as-was" condition before venturing a major redesign.

Appropriately coded *10 Blue*[5], the aircraft made its first flight on 20 May 1977 with distinguished test pilot[6] Vladimir S. Ilyushin at the controls. It was immediately apparent that the low AOA needed increasing to improve directional stability. Stage 1 of the test program centered on performance testing and evaluation of the integral layout, including high-alpha stability and handling. In the course of flight tests, the T10-1 was fitted with anti-flutter weights on the wings and fins near the tips. In this configuration the prototype flew well, making 38 flights by late January 1978 with various OKB test pilots.

Stage 2 FBW covered the controls and armament control system. The first prototype was donated to the Soviet Air Force Museum in Monino a few years after the definitive Su-27 entered production. The second prototype, T10-2, came out of Sukhoi's experimental shop in early 1978; it was almost identical. Unfortunately, the aircraft crashed on May 7 of the same year, killing test pilot Yevgeniy Solovyov.

Security measures taken during the prototype's construction were extremely tight, and very few OKB employees were granted access to the T10-1. (Sukhoi OKB archive)

The West got news of the T-10's existence when surveillance satellites photographed the aircraft in Zhukovskiy (then erroneously referred to as Ramenskoye in the West). Hence the aircraft was originally allocated the temporary ASCC reporting name Ram-K (Ram for Ramenskoye) since the manufacturer was unknown. The official designation Su-27 became known in 1982 and the reporting name was changed to Flanker.

The T10-1 in detail

The T10-1 is a twin-engine jet fighter of blended wing/body design; the wings and fuselage form a single lifting body.

Fuselage: The fuselage is made up of three subassemblies—forward, center, and rear fuselage. The forward fuselage incorporates the nose fairing, the pressurized cockpit with sliding canopy, the nose wheel well, and the LERXes. The nose fairing is made of metal and houses avionics and instrumentation.

The center fuselage incorporates the wing center-section, the forward integral fuel tank, the air intakes, the main-wheel wells, and fairings. The aft fuselage incorporates the engine bays, the center sections of the engine nacelles housing the inlet ducts, the stabilator attachment booms, and the central fuselage boom running between the engines. It terminates in a flattened "beaver tail" fairing between the nozzles.

Wings: Cantilever mid-wing of blended wing/body design, built in three sections (integral center section and two outer wings). The sharply swept LERXes blend smoothly into the outer wings to create an ogival wing. Leading-edge sweep on the outer wings is 41°. The wings are made up of sharp-nosed profiles with a variable thickness-to-chord ratio and have negative camber.

The trailing edge features one-piece ailerons and one-piece flaps.

The T10-1 under a special security shed at Sukhoi's test facility in Zhukovskiy. The shed protected the aircraft from U.S. surveillance satellites. (Sukhoi OKB archive)

Coded 10 Blue, the T10-1 entered flight test in the spring of 1977. (Sukhoi OKB archive)

This view clearly shows how far forward the nose gear unit was located on the first prototype. (Sukhoi OKB archive)

The outer wings have a three-spar structure with one-piece upper/lower skins and removable LE and wingtips. The wing torsion box contains integral fuel tanks. The three-section riveted wingtips are of complex curvature.

Tail unit: The T10-1 has differential stabilizers for pitch and roll control (stabilators). The trapezoidal stabilators have a leading-edge sweep of 45° and consist of five parts (forward, center, rear and root sections, and a tip fairing). The twin vertical tails are mounted on the engine nacelles. The trapezoidal fins have a two-spar structure with two main ribs at the root. The rudders are moved with hydraulic actuators within the fins. The dielectric fin tips house navigation and communications aerials.

Landing gear: The forward-retracting main units attached to the bottom of the wing center section have a breaker. During retraction the main-wheel rotates through 90° to lie horizontally in the wing root, enclosed by double doors; the forward door is hinged at the front and doubles as an airbrake.

The semi-levered suspension nose unit is attached to the forward bulkhead of the wheel well and retracts aft. It has a KN-27 non-braking wheel and a foreign object damage (FOD) guard. The forward door incorporates landing and taxi lights and the aft door opens to starboard.

Powerplant: Two Lyul'ka AL-21F-3 afterburning turbojets rated at 7,800 kgp (17,195 lb st) dry and 11,200 kgp (24,691 lb st) reheat. The engines feature an oxygen system for in-flight starting and afterburner ignition. Engines, afterburners, and accessories are cooled by ram-air intakes located dorsally on the stabilator attachment booms.

The engines are located in spaced nacelles on the fuselage

The T10-1 following modifications. Note the anti-flutter weights on the wings and fins. (Sukhoi OKB archive)

and ailerons have conventional mechanical controls while the stabilators have an analog FBW control system, providing adequate stability and control in yaw, pitch, and roll channels. In addition to the ailerons, roll control is exercised by differential deflection of the stabilators.

Hydraulics: Two separate systems with a pressure of 210 kg/cm^2 (3,000 psi).

Interceptor Prototypes T10-3 and T10-4

In 1978 the OKB began manufacturing the third prototype—the first Su-27 (T10-3)—to be powered by new-generation AL-31F engines. The new engines were shorter and of smaller diameter, featuring a new axisymmetric (convergent-divergent) nozzle and located ventrally, not dorsally as on the T10-1. This meant the engine nacelles had to be totally redesigned with a larger cross-section area, producing weight and SFC (specific fuel consumption) benefits.

Apart from the redesigned engine nacelles, the T10-3 differed from preceding prototypes in having outward-canted fins. Coded *310 Blue* (i.e., 3rd T-10), it was completed in 1979 and first flown on 23 August by Vladimir S. Ilyushin. This was also the first Su-27 with a gun.

Initially the T10-3 was used for engine testing. After completing its flight test program in 1982, the aircraft moved to Novofyodorovka airbase near the city of Saki on the Crimea peninsula, home to the AV-MF[7] Flight Test Center. OKB Nikolay F. Sadovnikov made the first takeoff from a provisional ski jump on 28 August. Takeoff weight was 18 tons (39,682 lbs.) and the takeoff run 200 m (656 ft.).

In 1983 the aircraft was fitted with an arrestor hook and re-coded *03 Blue*. The identical fourth prototype, T10-4, was built in parallel, making its

underside. They have rectangular-section adjustable supersonic air intakes with horizontal ramps and auxiliary blow-in doors. To prevent boundary layer ingestion, the intakes, attached to the fuselage by lugs, are set apart from the wing undersurface so that the intake upper lip acts as a boundary layer splitter plate.

Fuel system: The fuel system ensures stable operation of the engines throughout the flight envelope. It comprises five integral tanks—three in the fuselage and one in each outer wing. The forward and center-section fuel tanks are located in the center fuselage. The aft fuel tank is in the central boom between the engine nacelles. An automatic fuel management system ensures that the CG stays within prescribed limits as fuel is burned.

Control system: The T10-1 has a mixed control system. The rudders

first flight, with Vladimir S. Ilyushin, on 31 October 1979. This aircraft was used for armament and avionics trials.

Interceptor Prototypes T10-5, T10-6, T10-9, T10-10, and T10-11

To speed up the avionics test program, MAP tasked the Komsomol'sk-on-Amur factory with building a small pre-production batch of five T-10s. These were known as "type T10-5" but had individual designations, being the fifth, sixth, ninth, tenth, and eleventh prototypes—T10-5, T10-6, T10-9, T10-10, and T10-11.[8] The aircraft were something of a cross-breed between T10-1 and T10-3, being powered by AL-21F-3 turbojets but having outward-canted fins.

The pre-production aircraft differed in avionics fit, as each was assigned a different flight test program. T10-5 was the first to take to the air, making its first flight in June 1980; T10-6 followed in the same year. The remaining three were completed in 1981-82.

All five aircraft had eight weapons hardpoints. The shape of the dielectric radome varied from aircraft to aircraft; e.g., *51 Blue* and *10 Yellow* had sharply tapered noses à la T10-1, while the ninth and eleventh aircraft featured enlarged ogival

radomes quite similar to that of the definitive Su-27. The pitot boom was shorter on all five aircraft.

T10-S Interceptor

Tests of T10-1 and T10-3 showed that, in its original form, the fighter did not meet the specifications due to three main reasons. Firstly, it had failed the weight requirements. Secondly, they had been over optimistic regarding the SFC. Thirdly, the ogival wings and the placement of the vertical tails atop the engine nacelles did not give the T-10 an advantage over U.S. fighters in a dogfight.

Yevgeniy A. Ivanov, who succeeded Pavel O. Sukhoi as general designer, agreed with the chiefs of the VVS and MAP in demanding a redesign. The situation was so dire that Ivanov and Mikhail P. Simonov, who was appointed T-10 project chief in 1976, urged the engineers to bring in new ideas. For once the OKB leaders forgot their traditionally cautious approach; all ideas were welcome, even the most daring and "crazy" ones. Eight years of hard work were scrapped and a sort of in-house competition for the best layout ensued.

When working on the "second-generation" T-10, the engineers relied on foreign research, including

The T10-1 gets airborne for the first time. Footage of the first flight shown on Soviet TV created a sensation in the world's aviation circles. (Yefim Gordon archive)

Northrop's experience with LERXes on the F-20 Tigershark light fighter and the experimental YF-17. SibNIA drew up a list of airframe elements which could be changed. SibNIA tested numerous versions of the LERXes in its wind tunnels; the objective was to increase lift appreciably while creating a sufficiently high pitchdown force at any positive AOA.

One of the advantages of statically unstable aircraft with the CG located well aft (such as the T-10) is that the stabilators are deflected downwards at high alpha, augmenting wing lift at the expense of a slight increase in drag. However, in this case stabilator AOA exceeds wing AOA. This causes early airflow departure from the stabilators, decreasing the pitchdown force generated by them at full downward deflection and limiting the aircraft's alpha range. General Dynamics had experienced the same problem with the F-16.

Placing the CG further forward, making the aircraft statically stable, takes care of the problem. However, the advantages of the statically unstable layout were all-important for a fighter, so SibNIA engineers started looking for a compromise. Several unusual ways of increasing stabilator efficiency at high alpha were found in the course of wind-tunnel tests. SibNIA engineers proposed recontouring

The first prototype was donated to the Soviet Air Force Museum in Monino when the Su-27 entered production. (Yefim Gordon)

The fifth prototype, T10-5, reverted to the older AL-21F engines. The armament was very similar to the future production Su-27. (Sukhoi OKB archive)

After completing its initial flight test program, the T10-3 was modified under the Su-27K shipboard fighter development program and transferred to the naval test center at Saki AB for further trials. (Sukhoi OKB archive)

the wings and increasing wing area aft of the CG. Both Sukhoi and SibNIA were positive that the T-10 also needed leading-edge flaps to delay airflow departure from the wings. Wind-tunnel tests confirmed these decisions.

The main task now was to improve high-alpha handling. After more changes were made to the shape of the LERXes, the engineers began experimenting with LE flap deflection angles and, finally, the position of the vertical tails. The best solution, as it turned out, was to place the fins as far apart as possible. This improved the efficiency of both the vertical and horizontal tail. In a side wind at AOAs in excess of 20° the windward fin and rudder were always affected by the wake of the windward

wing, but the leeward fin and rudder stayed outside the turbulence, ensuring good directional control.

In 1976 a completely revamped T-10 project was developed under Simonov's leadership. An important new feature was the adaptive leading- and trailing-edge devices governed by the FBW control system. Hence the "T-10 Jr." entered the full-scale development stage. The result was the aircraft that we know today as Flanker, which gave rise to a whole family of excellent combat jets.

Research showed that the new wings indeed created a huge pitchdown force even with the stabilators deflected fully up; this later enabled the Su-27 to perform the famous "Cobra" maneuver

when the pilot retains full control at AOAs close to 120°.

Trials of the original T-10 revealed unacceptably intense vibration at AOAs exceeding 8°. A new and more precise method of predicting vibration levels was needed. For this an Su-9 interceptor (*61 Red*) with modified wings was converted under the T-4 bomber program. Results obtained confirmed the results of wind-tunnel tests. Additional pressure measurements on the redesigned T-10 wings in the T-203 tunnel showed that the new wing platform and recountoured LERXes reduced airflow pulsation dramatically, taking care of the vibration problem. The leading-edge flaps made a major contribution to this.

Other general arrangements of the T-10 were studied under Mikhail P. Simonov, including exotic ones with forward-swept wings and canard foreplanes. Numerous experiments were made with control surfaces and high-lift devices. A special rig was built to test air intake operation. The process of defining and refining continued. Research in the T-203 wind tunnel added up to 10,000 hours by 1985 – an impressive figure by any standards. T-10 models were also

There were actually five aircraft completed to T10-5 standard. The first one, the "real" T10-5, was coded 51 Blue *and sported an overall grayish-blue finish. (Sukhoi OKB archive)*

The 11th prototype, T10-11, immediately before touchdown. The shape of the ogival radome matches that of the production Su-27. (Sukhoi OKB archive)

When tests in Zhukovskiy were completed, the T10-11 was handed over to the NII VVS test center in Akhtoobinsk. (Sukhoi OKB archive)

tested in the T-205M transonic tunnel and T-313 supersonic tunnel.

Finally, the Sukhoi OKB began issuing working drawings for the redesigned fighter and prepared for prototype construction. To distinguish it from the original T-10 the aircraft was designated T10-S, the suffix letter standing for *sereeynyy*—production. The T10-S bore only a slight resemblance to its predecessor. Wing area was increased from 59.4 m² (638.7 sq. ft.) to 62.04 m² (667.09 sq. ft.) in order to decrease wing loading during takeoff and aerial combat. The ogival wings became more traditional with a straight LE outboard of the LERXes. They terminated in missile launch rails, increasing the number of hardpoints to ten; these doubled as anti-flutter weights and were only a fraction heavier than the weights used on the T10-1.

The wings used a new and flatter airfoil. The fixed cambered LE of the early prototypes was replaced by full-span leading-edge flaps, while the separate ailerons and flaps were supplanted by one-piece flaperons. The new wings created less drag, despite the bigger area, and gave higher lift in cruise, maneuvering and takeoff/landing modes. They also afforded better lateral stability and roll control.

To reduce drag, the canopy cross-section was reduced and its aft portion flattened. The fuselage cross-section was reduced ahead of the cockpit area, but increased aft where the

forward fuel tank was located. The radius of the blended wing/fuselage fairings was increased and the fairings extended aft. The engines had dorsally-mounted accessories. This reduced maximum overall cross-section and surface area, decreasing both drag and specific airframe weight. The air intakes incorporated retractable FOD protection grilles and ventral blow-in doors.

To improve directional control at high alpha, the fins were moved outboard to the stabilator attachment

booms and disposed vertically, not canted outwards; this again reduced surface area and cross-section. The fins were placed further forward than on the original T-10, the anti-flutter weights on the horizontal tail had been deleted, so for better flutter resistance the stabilator hinges were moved forward along the chord. Directional stability and spinning characteristics were improved by fitting ventral fins to the tail unit attachment booms.

The new main gear was simpler, lighter, and more compact. It featured

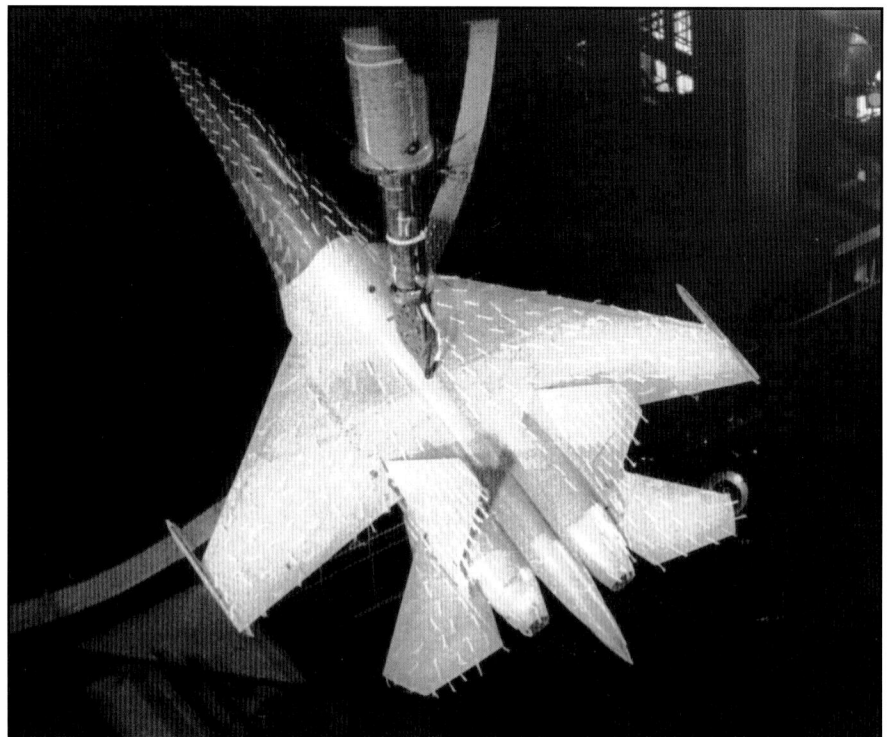

A model of the T-10 (incorporating modifications based on early test flights) in the TsAGI wind tunnel in Zhukovskiy. The refined aerodynamics allowed the fighter's performance to be improved perceptibly. (Sukhoi OKB archive)

WARBIRDTECH
SERIES

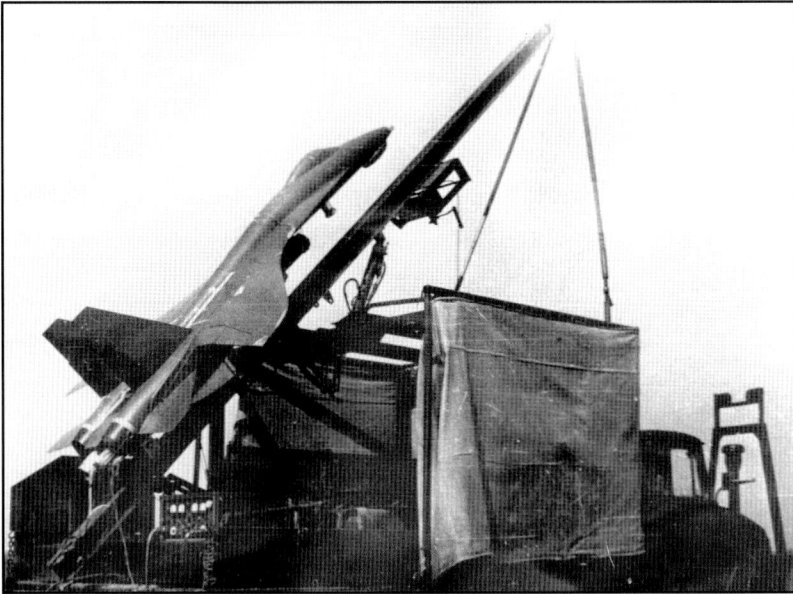

Left and Above: A scale model of the T10-S fired from a special catapult. (Yefim Gordon)

The T10-15 was almost identical to the production Su-27. (Yefim Gordon archive)

skewed retraction hinges instead of breaker struts so that the wheels turned through 90° during retraction without the aid of any mechanical linkage. The nose unit retracted forward and was closed by a single door. A single large dorsal airbrake was located immediately aft of the cockpit *à la* F-15, which caused no change in pitch trim when deployed. The aft fuselage was redesigned, the flat "beaver tail" of the early prototypes giving way to a characteristic circular-section "stinger" extending beyond the engine nozzles. This housed the brake chute container and the aft fuel tank, allowing for pitch trim as fuel was consumed.

The combined effect of these changes reduced airframe drag 18 to 20% in both subsonic and supersonic mode. The overall cross-section was reduced, while the internal fuel load

had grown by 500 kg (1,102 lbs.). The integral layout provided a major increase in lift at high alpha and enhanced maneuverability. The airframe was fairly lightweight, utilizing new high-strength titanium and aluminum alloys and state-of-the-art manufacturing technologies, and was stressed for +9 G. The design stage was finally completed in 1980, the same year OKB's experimental shop started manufacturing three prototypes of the T10-S.

Interceptor Prototypes T10-7, T10-8, and T10-12

The first Su-27 as we know it, T10-S, was actually the seventh Su-27 prototype; hence it was designated T10-7. It was completed in early 1981, making its first flight on 20 April with test pilot Vladimir S. Ilyushin.

Outwardly, *27 Blue* was not quite a production-standard Flanker. Being intended for handling, performance, and powerplant testing, the T10-7 lacked armament and mission avionics, including radar, so it had a non-standard short conical radome borrowed from the early prototypes. Unfortunately, the aircraft's career was brief. On 3 September 1981 the T10-7 suffered a critical failure at the end of a test flight. Ilyushin ejected safely but the aircraft was destroyed.

Designated T10-12, the second flying T10-S was rolled out in the same year; this aircraft featured a representative fire control system. Unfortunately, the second aircraft didn't last long either. On 23 December

An utterly unique photo of five different Su-27 prototypes lined up on the ramp in Akhtoobinsk. Left to right: T10-15, T10-27, T10-10, T10-11 and T10-16. (Sukhoi OKB archive)

The T10-22 also participated in the state acceptance trials. (Sukhoi OKB archive)

The T10-17 was the "standard-setter" for the production Su-27, differing only in having straight-cropped fin tips. The bright blue color scheme, on the other hand, was unusual. (Sukhoi OKB archive)

A still from a once classified ciné film shot for top MoD officials showing the T10-27. The aircraft has a non-standard short radome reminiscent of the early prototypes. (Sukhoi OKB archive)

Air-to-air shot of the T10-17 during state acceptance trials. (Sukhoi OKB archive)

The T10-17 was used for the state acceptance trials of the T10-S version, becoming a workhorse for the test pilots. (Sukhoi OKB archive)

1981 it crashed, killing test pilot A. Komarov; the forward fuselage broke up in high-speed flight at altitude. A further T10-S – the static test airframe designated T10-8 – was built in 1982; the static test program was completed the same year. By then further prototypes of the T10-S were flying and trials were going smoothly.

In late 1982 the aircraft entered production in Komsomol'sk-on-Amur and achieved initial operational capability (IOC) with the IA PVO and the VVS. The version for the IA PVO was designated Su-27P (*perekhvatchik* – interceptor), while the VVS version was known simply as the Su-27. A total of 14 development aircraft, including static test airframes, participated in the manufacturer's trials program. In its production form it was code-named Flanker-B, the original prototype becoming the Flanker-A.

Development Aircraft T10-15, T10-17, T10-18, and T10-22

Four initial production aircraft were used in the state acceptance trials program and systems and armament trials. These were T10-15 (coded *15 Yellow*), T10-17 (*17 Blue*), T10-18 (*18 Blue*), and T10-22 (*22 Blue*). These aircraft looked every bit like production-standard Su-27s, except for the dielectric fin caps which were lopped off horizontally; their shape was to change before long.

17 Blue bore the brunt of the state acceptance trials program, including live firing trials. It sported a non-standard paint job: the pale blue forward fuselage contrasted sharply with the deep blue of the wings, upper fuselage, vertical tail, and air intakes.

The T10-18 was the first Su-27 to be used in the strike role, dropping free-fall bombs. The T10-22 gained the distinction of being the first Su-27 to be displayed to the general public at Khodynka airfield in central Moscow in August 1989; this aircraft now resides in the VVS Museum in Monino.

T10-20R Record-breaker Aircraft

An early-production aircraft coded *20 Blue*, the T10-20 (c/n 36911005705, f/n 0505)[9], was later modified for a world speed record attempt on a 500 km (310.5 mile) closed circuit after completing its trials program. The modified aircraft was redesignated T10-20R for *rekordnyy* – record-breaking. However, the record-breaking flight was never made and *20 Blue* was retired to Khodynka.

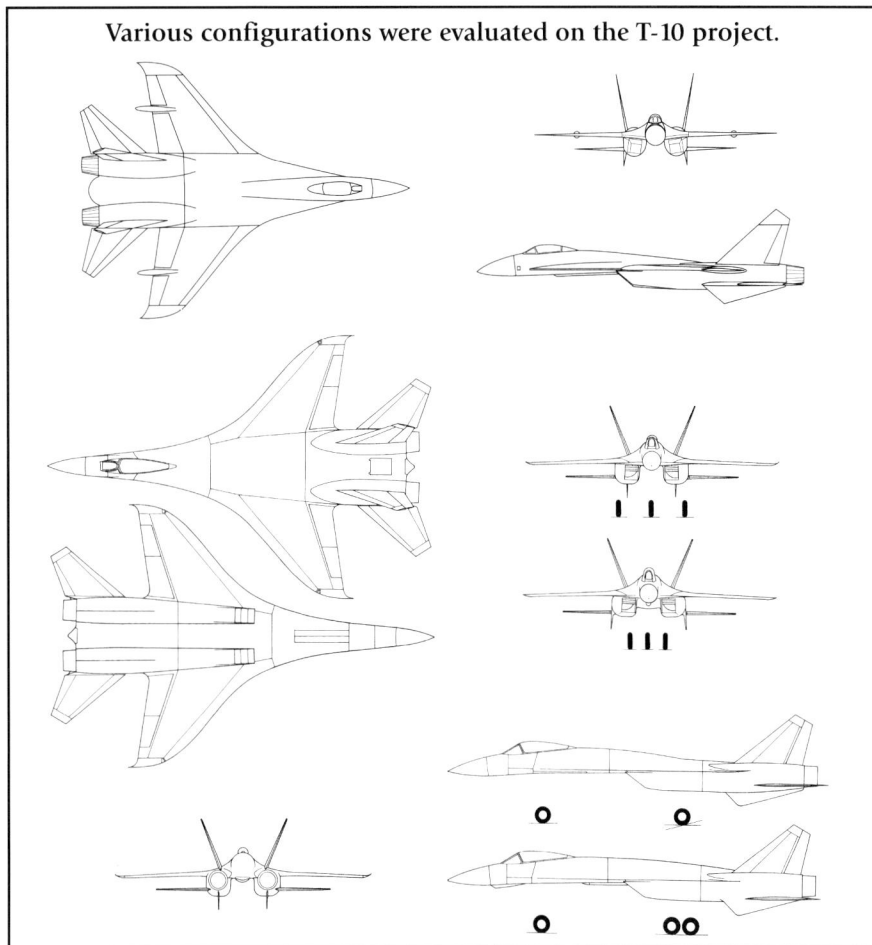

Various configurations were evaluated on the T-10 project.

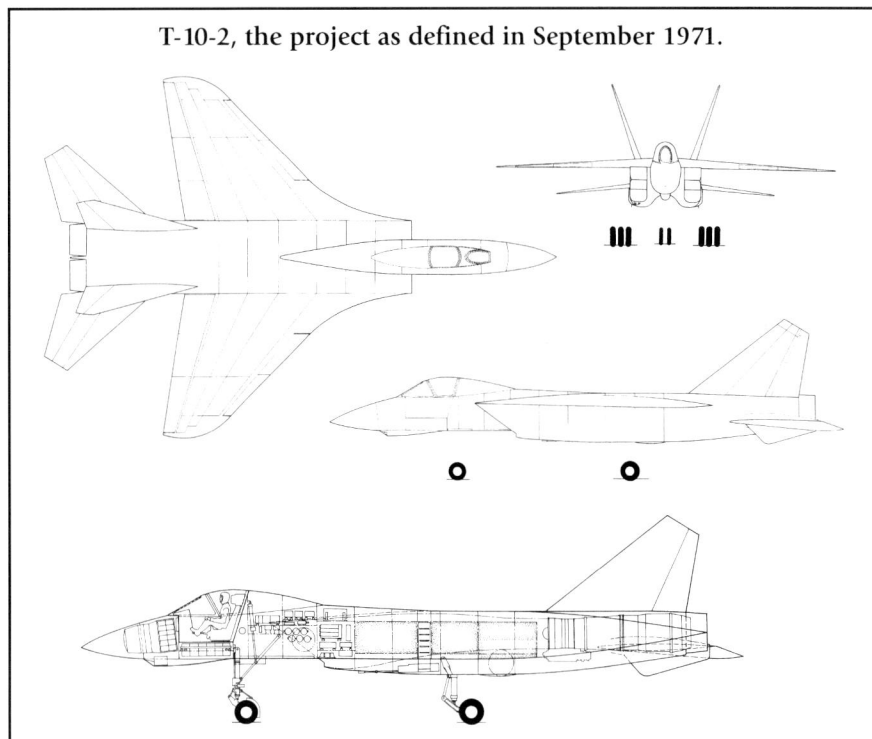

T-10-2, the project as defined in September 1971.

PRODUCTION VERSIONS

A production Su-27 built in Komsomol'sk-on-Amur. (Yefim Gordon)

Interceptor Su-27P (T10-S)

The high performance of the production Su-27 was due to a number of new technologies. These included some world firsts:

- Load-bearing airframe components made of high-strength titanium automatically arc-welded in a liquid medium (e.g., fuselage mainframes, wing fittings, stabilator spars, etc.);
- Structural components made of high-strength titanium sheets (corrugated walls in the wing center section integral fuel tank, tail unit attachment beams and FOD grilles) manufactured by automated dual-arc welding;
- Welded titanium structural components with a high-quality surface finish obtained by using a new technology (fixed-temperature annealing). The large-scale use of high-strength titanium resulted not only in a substantial weight saving, but also in a high-quality surface finish;
- FOD screens with 2.5 to 2.5 mm apertures made by electric erosion (100,000 channels angled at 30° with divider walls 0.5 mm thick).

To speed up deliveries, the factory began preparing for production while tests progressed and had full-scale production going as early as 1982. This was a risk that paid off. Early deliveries were targeted at the IA PVO; the VVS had to wait until later. Soon, however, a series of accidents forced Sukhoi engineers to take action. The second T10-S (T10-12) suffered structural failure at high speed. Later, in a similar accident, the wing failed. The leading-edge flap and part of the outer wing disintegrated during a low-level, high-speed dash. Luckily, Sadovnikov managed to land the crippled aircraft in one piece minus the outer wing and half a fin, enabling the engineers to eliminate the cause.

A number of improvements were made at an early stage. The radome's diameter was increased and its length increased by 680 mm (2 ft. 2.77 in.); this reduced the pilot's downward field of view by a mere 1°. Some early production batches had the forward fuselage reinforced with external plates. Later aircraft had the forward fuselage structure beefed up and these plates removed.

A transverse frame member was added to the canopy to ease production. For better fatigue resistance, the original straight dielectric fin caps were replaced by raked ones and the anti-flutter weights were deleted. In mid 1987 the tail "stinger" was lengthened and widened to accommodate APP-50 chaff/flare dispensers (*apparaht postanovki pomekh*). Steel reinforcement plates were added to the stabilators as a safety measure should a missile drop from an inboard pylon and strike the stabilator.

The AL-31F engines also received upgrades. The most important ones were the introduction of a turned main combustion chamber with welded fuel manifolds, a reinforced high-pressure (HP) turbine disc, new specially coated HP turbine blades, and improved bearings.

Production Su-27Ps were fitted with a Phazotron (NIIR) N-001 "Mech" (Sword) coherent pulse-Doppler fire control radar, codenamed *Slot Back* by NATO. It had "look-down/shoot-down" capability, detecting and tracking up to ten targets below the fighter's own flight level, assigning the two top-priority

Su-27s under production at KnaAPO. (Yefim Gordon archive)

27/C8: An early production Su-27 at the NII VVS test centre in Akhtoobinsk. (Sukhoi OKB archive)

85 Red was one of the first production Su-27s delivered to NII VVS. This aircraft is still fully operational. (Sukhoi OKB archive)

threats among the targets and guiding AAMs to them, even in an electronic countermeasures (ECM) environment.

The OEPS-27 optoelectronic sighting system (*optiko-elektronnaya preetsel'naya sistema*) featured an infrared search and track (IRST) unit with day and night channels and a laser rangefinder, enabling the aircraft to attack covertly. This was linked to an NSTs-27 helmet-mounted sight (*nashlemnaya sistema tseleookazahniya* – HMS).

The Su-27P featured a "Biryuza" command link system (Turquoise; pronounced *biryoozah*) enabling ground centers to direct the aircraft by feeding data via a secure link. For the first time on a Soviet combat aircraft, a united communications suite was installed, facilitating concerted action by groups of aircraft.

The production Su-27P was equipped with a single-barrel 30 mm (1.18 caliber) GSh-301 gun in the starboard LERX. It used the AO-18 round and had a rate of fire of 1,600 rpm with 150 rounds. The aircraft also had ten wing and fuselage pylons for air-to-air missiles.

Multi-role Fighter Su-27 (Su-27S, T10-S)

Production T10-S fighters delivered to the VVS have a secondary strike role. Their extended weaponry includes 100 kg (220 lbs.), 250 kg (551 lbs.) and 500 kg (1,102 lbs.) free-fall bombs and various unguided rockets.

To enhance defensive capability, the tail "stinger" was modified to house additional APP-50 chaff/flare dispensers, bringing the total number of flares to 96. Late-production Su-27s feature an upgraded N-001 radar capable of guiding AAMs to two targets at a time. Two pylons were added under the outer wings, increasing the number of hardpoints to 12 and the ordnance load from 6,000 kg

A port-side view of 85 Red, an operational Su-27s. (Sukhoi OKB archive)

This early production Su-27, 14 Red, was operated by LII for pilot training for a long time until lost in a fatal crash during an airshow in Salgareda, Italy. (Yefim Gordon)

The T10-24 during assembly at the OKB's experimental plant. (Sukhoi OKB archive)

Two views of the T10-26 development aircraft. (Sukhoi OKB archive)

The T10-24 made numerous takeoffs from the ski jump at Saki AB to check the use of canards on a shipboard version of the Su-27. The results proved encouraging. (Sukhoi OKB archive)

Rollout of the T10-26. (Sukhoi OKB archive)

The T10-26 had an unusually long pitot boom and was used by LII in various research programs for a long time. (Sukhoi OKB archive)

(13,227 lbs.) to 8,000 kg (17,636 lbs.); this necessitated a reinforcement of the main gear oleos to cater for a TOW (Tube-launched, Optically tracked, Wire-guided missile) increased to 33,000 kg (72,751 lbs.).

Control Configured Vehicle T10-24

The idea of fitting canard foreplanes to the Su-27 dated back to 1977, before the T10-S had flown. However, tunnel tests showed the canards would cause pitch-control problems at certain AOAs. It took five years to cure this problem. The canards were positioned on the LERXes just aft of the cockpit; they had a span of 6.4 m (21 ft.), an area of approximately 3 m² (32.25 sq. ft.), and a leading-edge sweep of 53° 30 ft.

The first Flanker to be equipped with canards, the T10-24 (*24 Blue*), was completed and flown in May 1985. It was used for aerodynamics research. Tests showed that the canards improved field performance and high-alpha handling; they assisted when the stabilators found themselves in the wake of the wings at certain AOAs and became inefficient. The canards were programmed to deflect automatically as the angle of attack grew; they increased static instability and lift.

Development Aircraft T10-25

Another early-production Su-27, the T10-25 (*25 Blue*), was modified under the Su-27K development program. This aircraft, fitted with an arrestor hook, was used to investigate and practice carrier operations, making ski jump takeoffs and arrestor-wire engagements in the Crimea. Its first flight probably took place on 3 August 1984 flown by Nikolay F. Sadovnikov. The aircraft also differed from production Su-27s in having

Viktor Pugachov about to take off on another training flight before the official record attempt. (Sukhoi OKB archive)

straight-cropped fin tips *à la* T10-7 and sported the Soviet Navy's blue and white flag under the cockpit.

Development Aircraft T10-26

The 14th production aircraft, T10-26 (*26 Blue*), became a flight test workhorse at LII, which used it, among other things, for spinning trials. Outward recognition features included a white radome, a non-standard nose pitot and spin recovery rockets under the wings.

The P-42 was a record-breaking aircraft converted from the T10-15 prototype. (Yefim Gordon)

Record-breaker Aircraft P-42 (T10-15 Mod)

In late 1986 many papers and magazines published reports of a new series of time-to-height records set by a Soviet aircraft enigmatically designated P-42. Between 1986 and 1988 this aircraft had claimed a total of 27 time-to-height and sustained altitude records. To have them duly registered by the FAI (International Aeronautics Federation), the Soviet Union had to supply data on the aircraft's power-plant; and so it did, stating officially that the P-42 was powered by two equally enigmatic "R-32 jet engines rated at 13,600 kgp" (29,982 lb st).

The main idea of the record attempts was to find out what the Su-27 could really do and confirm its

WARBIRDTECH
S E R I E S

The LMK-2405 was displayed at all major airshows in Zhukovskiy – MosAeroShow '92, MAKS '93, MAKS '95 and MAKS '97. (Yefim Gordon)

The T10U-1 trainer prototype as originally completed with the non-standard fin tips. The first two were converted from single-seaters. It first flew on 7 March 1985. (Sukhoi OKB archive)

The wheel brakes could not hold the P-42 with the engines running at full power, so the aircraft had to be linked to a special mobile restraint. (Sukhoi OKB archive)

superiority over the F-15—thereby boosting national prestige. Simonov spoke true: the aircraft chosen for the mission was indeed a standard-production Su-27; however, it was extensively modified to reduce weight.

The radar was removed and the radome replaced by a lightweight metal fairing. The large dorsal airbrake and its actuator were removed. The LE flaps and flaperons were replaced by fixed leading and trailing edges, leaving only the stabilators for roll control. The brake chute container was deleted and the tail "stinger" shortened. The internal gun and missile pylons were removed, as were the dielectric fin caps, ventral fins, and nosewheel mudguard.

The "R-32" engines were in fact AL-31Fs modified to increase thrust

in full afterburner to 13,598 kgp (29,978 lb st), adding more than 1,000 kgp (2,204 lb st); the movable air intake ramps were fixed at the optimum setting. The avionics and communications suite was reduced to safe limits and the aircraft was stripped of paint to save weight. The combined effect of these measures reduced the MTOW (maximum take-off weight) to 14,100 kg (31,084 lbs.). This and the uprated engines gave an unparalleled thrust-to-weight ratio of 1.93, enabling the P-42 to pass Mach 1 in a vertical climb.

The first post-conversion flight took place on February 25, 1986. By autumn the aircraft (officially designated P-42) was ready. On October 27 and November 15 Sukhoi test pilot Viktor G. Pugachov set no less

than eight time-to-height records—four absolute world records in the landplane class and four in the 12,000-16,000 kg (26,455-35,273 lb) MTOW class, reaching 3 km (9,842 ft.) in 25.573 seconds, 6 km (19,685 ft.) in 37.05 seconds. During the record flights the P-42 flew with only barely enough fuel to climb to the required altitude and return home.

More records followed on 10 March 1987 and 23 March 1988, when Nikolay Sadovnikov climbed to 9 km (29,527 ft.) in 44 seconds, 12 km (39,370 ft.) in 55.2 seconds, and 15 km (49,212 ft.) in 70.329 seconds. Thus the P-42 beat the records set by the F-15 at Grand Forks AFB, North Dakota, on 16 January 1975 when it climbed to 3 km in 27.5 seconds, reached 6, 9, and 12 km in

39.33 seconds, 48.86 seconds, and 59.38 seconds, respectively, and climbed to 15 km in 77.02 seconds. The aircraft in question had been a similarly lightened F-15A christened *Streak Eagle*. On 10 June 1987 Sadovnikov set a Class N world record of altitude in sustained flight – 19,337 m (63,441 ft.). The last record set by the P-42 with Pugachov at the controls involved climbing to 15 km in 81.71 seconds with a 1,000 kg (2,204 lb) payload.

The P-42's immense thrust-to-weight ratio immediately created a problem: the brakes could not hold it at maximum thrust. Sukhoi quickly found a solution – the aircraft was attached to a heavy bulldozer. A massive steel plate acting as a jet blast deflector was fitted to protect the driver. After engaging full afterburner, the pilot disconnected the restraining cable. Ciné cameras and chronometers were switched on at the same moment, and the aircraft leaped forward, climbing away vertically after a very short run.

Further record attempts with the P-42 had to be put on hold in the late '80s due to economic problems. The aircraft still survives at Zhukovskiy.

Display Aircraft Su-27PD

The second of the two Su-27Ps donated to Anatoliy Kvochur's "Istrebeeteli" (Fighters) aerobatic team was retrofitted with a retractable refueling probe and redesignated Su-27PD, the D standing for *dozapravka* (refueling). This aircraft, coded *598 White* (c/n 36911037820, f/n 3720), was the only land-based single-seat T10-S to have flight refueling.

Multi-role Export Fighter Su-27SK

An export version of the Su-27 (T10-S) for China and Vietnam was designated Su-27SK. "S" stands for

81 Red, *a very early production* sparka, *was delivered to NII VVS in Akhtoobinsk for trials. (Sukhoi OKB archive)*

The T10U-1 with modified fin tips identical to those of production Su-27s. (Sukhoi OKB archive)

The Su-27UB's tandem cockpits are enclosed by a single canopy. (Yefim Gordon)

sereeynyy (production), while "K" stands for *kommehrcheskiy* (commercial). The Su-27SK has a reinforced landing gear, a MTOW increased to 33,000 kg (72,751 lbs.), and slightly downgraded avionics. Foreign avionics may be installed at the customer's request.

The Su-27SK entered production in 1991. Deliveries to China's People's Liberation Army Air Force (PLAAF) began in 1992.

Multi-role Export Fighter Su-27SMK

A more capable version of the Su-27SK was developed as the Su-27SMK, the "M" standing for *modernizeerovannyy* (upgraded). Changes include two extra hardpoints under the outer wings increasing the ordnance load to 8,000 kg (17,636 lbs.), improved targeting, navigation, communications and ECM equipment, two "wet" pylons permitting the carriage of 2,000 lit.

(440 Imp. gal) drop tanks, and a retractable refueling probe. It features an improved version of the N-001 pulse-Doppler fire-control radar. Western avionics and/or weapons may be integrated at customer request.

Modified "Roosskiye Vityazi" Su-27

After the Cam Ranh tragedy of 1995, when three Su-27s of the "Roosskiye Vityazi" (Russian Knights) aerobatic team crashed into a hillside in poor weather, killing the crews, six new aircraft were delivered to the team in 1996 fitted with GPS and upgraded comms equipment.

LMK-2405 CCV

Flankers were widely used as research aircraft and systems testbeds. One such aircraft was revealed at MosAeroShow '92 in Zhukovskiy when LII displayed a Su-27 coded *05*

Red. Outwardly this was virtually a standard Flanker. Yet it was a CCV, a part of the LMK-2405 active flight safety research complex[10] developed for testing-control techniques for future high-maneuverability fighters. It featured an advanced digital FBW control system with a sidestick and a full-authority digital engine control (FADEC) system.

Special multi-faceted angle reflectors were fitted under the wingtip missile rails to give a better radar signature. Flight and systems data were transmitted to the ground in real time by an omnidirectional telemetry system with aerials aft of the cockpit and beneath the port air intake. The aircraft could be fitted with spin recovery rockets under the wings.

Su-27 Thrust-Vectoring Nozzle Testbed

To increase the agility of new-generation fighters NPO "Saturn" (as the Lyul'ka OKB is now known) developed a movable axisymmetric convergent-divergent nozzle with thrust vectoring. A prototype nozzle underwent a long bench-testing program in 1987.

Next year the Sukhoi OKB and NPO "Saturn" converted an Su-27 for thrust vectoring control (TVC) research. Only one engine had a movable nozzle, the other one was standard. Flight tests began in 1989 and confirmed that the movable nozzle improved maneuverability, especially at low speeds.

A side view of a production Su-27UB with the closed canopy (Yefim Gordon)

Combat-Capable Trainer Su-27UB (T10-U)

Work on a trainer version of the T-10 designated T10-U (*oochebnyy* – training) began in the late '70s with detailed design completed in 1980. The Su-27UB was designated UB – *oochebno-boyevoy* [*samolyot*] – combat-capable trainer.

40% of the Su-27UB's fuselage ahead of the wings and 70% of the upper fuselage (above the wing center section) were new. The rear seat was raised to improve instructor visibility; the downward field of view from the back seat was an unprecedented 6°. This arrangement provided room for two avionics bays under the rear seat. The cockpits were enclosed by a common aft-hinged canopy, shortening ejection time. The airbrake was reshaped and slightly enlarged. The outer wings had 5% greater thickness-to-chord ratio at the tips. The nose gear unit was reinforced due to the heavier forward fuselage.

To compensate for the added side area ahead of the CG, the fins were lengthened with a 420 mm (16.53 in.) plug at the root. This increased the fin area by 20%. Systems changes included more oxygen for the second crew member, a modified air conditioning system, electrics, and dual controls. These changes added 1,500 kg (3,306 lbs.) to the Su-27UB's MTOW.

The trainee's and instructor's cockpits with the canopy open. (Sukhoi Design Bureau)

WARBIRD**TECH**
S E R I E S

Upon completion of its flight test program, the second prototype Su-27UB (T10U-2) was converted into the Aircraft 02-10 flight refueling system testbed. (Sukhoi OKB archive)

Aircraft 02-10 during a long-range test flight. This refueling systems testbed was converted from the second prototype UB trainer in 1985. In June 1987 this enabled it to fly non-stop from Moscow to Komsomol'sk-on-Amur with in-flight refueling. (Sukhoi OKB archive)

A static test airframe was built in 1984 and tests continued well into 1985. Designated T10U-1, the first prototype was first flown on 7 March 1985.

The second prototype, T10U-2 (*02 Blue*), joined the test program the same year, followed by the T10U-3 in 1986. The aircraft successfully passed the manufacturer's flight test and state acceptance trials programs and was cleared for production. The ASCC code name for the trainer was Flanker-C.

The first two prototypes had been built by KnaAPO – converted from early single-seaters (hence the straight fin caps of the T10U-1). Full-scale production was assigned to a different plant – aircraft factory No. 125 in Irkutsk, now named IAPO.[11] The first production Su-27UB took off on 10 September 1986.

Operational experience with the *sparka*,[12] as the Su-27UB was informally known, proved that the maximum commonality idea worked; the results of the trials (including high-alpha trials) and pilots' impressions were good. This was effectively demonstrated when an Su-27UB belonging to the Lipetsk conversion training center paid a visit to Langley AFB, Virginia. Col. A. Kharchevskiy and Maj. Ye. Karabasov came out on top in mock combat with the F-15D.

Export Trainer Su-27UBK

An export version of the trainer designated Su-27UBK to match the export single-seat fighter was soon developed – largely by IAPO's own design bureau. The aircraft differs slightly from the Su-27UB in avionics fit and weapons range. A small number of them were delivered to China and Vietnam.

Refueling Systems Test Bed "Aircraft 02-10"

In 1985 the Sukhoi OKB experimentally fitted the second Su-27UB prototype (*02 Blue*) with a retractable refueling probe to test the Su-27K's flight refueling system and investigate crew workloads and physical condition on long missions.

The carefully designed cockpit of the Su-27UB, together with the refueling capability, greatly increased mission time. In June 1987 it made an unprecedented non-stop flight across the country. In March 1988 the same aircraft flew from Moscow to Komsomol'sk-on-Amur and back, covering 13,440 km (7,466 nm) in 15 hrs 42 min.

The next modification involved the addition of an arrestor hook under the tail "stinger," just like on the T10-25. It also served as an avionics testbed for the "Resistor" automatic carrier landing system and a tanker for the first prototype Su-27K (T10K-1), transferring fuel by means of an UPAZ-1A "buddy" refueling pod.[13]

Thrust Vectoring Test Bed Su-27UB-PS

At an early stage of its thrust vectoring research, the Sukhoi OKB modified a Su-27UB coded *08 Blue*, fitting a long structure terminating in a two-dimensional movable nozzle (reminiscent of the F-15S/MTD testbed) to the port engine. The aircraft was unofficially referred to as the Su-27UB-PS for *plos*koye *sop*lo – "flat (i.e., two-dimensional) nozzle."

Aircraft 02-10 clearing the ski jump at Saki AB. (Sukhoi OKB archive)

Later, Aircraft 02-10 was fitted with an arrestor hook under the Su-27K development program. (Sukhoi OKB archive)

*The Sukhoi OKB converted this Su-27UB, 08 Blue, into a combined propulsion systems testbed/CCV for thrust vectoring research. The aircraft was known unofficially as the Su-27UB-PS (*plos*koye *sop*lo – "flat," meaning two-dimensional nozzle). (Yefim Gordon)*

WARBIRD**TECH**
S E R I E S

A NEW GENERATION OF FLANKERS

Air Superiority Fighter Su-35 (Su-27M, T10-M)

Chronologically the first of the Su-30 series to fly, this fighter started life as the T10-M or Su-27M (*modernizeerovannyy* – upgraded) before the service designation was changed to Su-35. The design effort led by chief project engineer Nikolay F. Nikitin was one of the greatest challenges for the OKB. The most obvious new feature was the addition of canards that had been tested on the T10-24 CCV. The canards made the aircraft more agile, especially at AoAs around 120°. The canards directed the vortices in such a way as to delay airflow separation from the wings and horizontal tail. Besides increasing lift during sharp maneuvers in a dogfight, this virtually eliminated high-alpha buffeting which caused control problems and made weapons aiming difficult on previous versions of the Su-27.

This allowed the T10-M to pull 10 Gs briefly without requiring structural reinforcement and hence incurring a weight penalty. Trim drag in supersonic cruise was also reduced. The T10-M was the world's first fighter to incorporate the automatic spin prevention/recovery feature.

Apart from the canards, the Su-27M (T10-M) differed from the standard Su-27 (T10-S) in a number of respects. First, the standard AL-31F engines rated at 12,500 kgp (27,557 lb st) in full afterburner were replaced by experimental AL-31FMs uprated to 12,800 kgp (28,218 lb st). Second, for better directional stability the T10-M had taller vertical tails of increased area and thickness with horizontally

The first prototype (T10M-1), coded 701 Black outline, during trials at NII VVS in Akhtoobinsk. Most Su-27M prototypes had low-visibility tactical codes. The first prototype sported an unusual three-tone grey camouflage, as Sukhoi kept experimenting with camouflage schemes for the production Su-35. (Yefim Gordon archive)

cropped tips made of carbon fiber reinforced plastic (CFRP) and incorporated integral fuel tanks.

The weapons control system (WCS) was new, comprising a more powerful multi-mode fire-control

The T10M-1 at Sukhoi's test facility in Zhukovskiy. The aircraft was relegated to the Monino museum shortly afterwards. (Yefim Gordon)

The T10M-1 at Monino museum parked beneath the massive twin rotor Mi-12 helicopter. (Marcus Fulber)

modes automated as much as possible. For the first time on a Soviet fighter, the aircraft had an electronic flight instrumentation system (EFIS) or "glass cockpit" featuring color liquid-crystal multi-function displays (MFDs). The avionics suite was built around a high-speed processor which took care of various tasks – from mission plan entry to weapons control – by utilizing typical combat scenarios stored in its memory to give the required information and "hints" to the pilot.

The incline of the K-36DM ejection seat was increased to 30°, easing the effect of G loads. The built-in test equipment (BITE) reduced preparation time and the need for ground support equipment. The capacity of the oxygen system was increased, and food, water, and waste containers were provided for long sorties.

All ten prototypes, T10M-1 through T10M-10, were coded 701 through 710 and built by KnAAPO, but not all were newly built aircraft. Wearing the low-visibility tactical code *701 Black* outline, the first prototype was converted from a standard T10-S built in 1986.

The second prototype (T10M-2, coded 702) – also a converted Flanker-B – joined the test program in January 1989. The next aircraft, T10M-3 (*703 Blue* outline), took off on 1 April 1992. This was the first Su-27M

radar. This required a re-contoured radome that was of true ogival shape and was not tipped with a pitot. A new radar homing and warning system (RHAWS) was installed, and the aircraft had a retractable refueling probe offset to port. Finally, two additional pylons were fitted under the inner wings, increasing the hardpoints to 12 and the ordnance to 8,000 kg (17,636 lb).

Sukhoi paid special attention to improving working conditions for the pilot, with all flight and combat

The third prototype Su-27M (T10M-3, 703 Blue outline) in Zhukovskiy during trials, the FBW canards acted like leading edge slats and could be set at +10 to –50 degrees dependant on the AOA. (Sukhoi OKB)

703 Blue *following repaint in a splinter camouflage. The vivid colors of the disruptive camouflage scheme make the aircraft a little bit more impressive. (Yefim Gordon)*

The Su-35 differs from the basic Su-27 mainly in having ground-attack capability. Here, a Kh-31P anti-radiation missile is carried beneath the Su-27M's wing. (Yefim Gordon)

(Su-35) to be built as such; it was also the first example to have the intended tall square-tipped fins, twin-wheel nose gear, and IFR capability.

The Su-27Ms had detail differences. For example, the first, second, sixth, and seventh aircraft were converted Su-27s; hence they had standard short vertical tails and single-wheel nose-gear units. This suggested that the N-011 radar was not fitted to these aircraft. The other six prototypes (703 through 705 and 708 through 710) had twin-wheel nose gear units and tall CFRP fins with squared-off tips and integral tanks. Additionally, the newly built Su-27Ms featured bigger fuel tanks in the wing torsion box. This increased the internal fuel load to 10,250 kg (22,597 lb).

Soon after the Su-27M's Machoolischchi debut, it was decided to show the new fighter to the outside world. By then the aircraft had been designated Su-35 to emphasize how different it was from the production Su-27 – and possibly to gain more funding. The Su-35 raised a few eyebrows at the Farnborough International '92 by appearing with a Ferranti thermal imaging and airborne laser device (TIALD). This was probably the first time a Russian combat aircraft came with Western avionics.

At Farnborough International '92, the T10M-3 still wore the standard two-tone blue camouflage applied to Soviet Air Force Su-27s.

The Su-35 has slightly larger vertical tails with horizontally cropped tips. The number 350 is likely to be an exhibitor number for the Paris Air Show. (Eero Saarela)

The Su-35's instrument panel. The third multi-function color LCD is offset to starboard. (Yefim Gordon)

The following year, however, it was repainted in a striking three-tone disruptive camouflage with two vivid shades of blue and light grey. The ninth prototype, T10M-9 (*709 Blue*) later received a similar splinter scheme but in "tropical" shades of tan, leaf green and chocolate brown (and became *709 Black* outline). These two aircraft were intended for overseas demonstrations, hence the odd paint jobs.

In 1993 the T10M-3 appeared at IDEX '93 in Dubai in its new colors. Accompanied by the Su-30MK prototype (*603 Black* outline), the Su-35 arrived in Dubai under its own power. The Su-30MK put on a lively aerobatics display including elements that could give the pilot a decisive dogfight advantage – the trademark Pugachov Cobra and the unfamiliar Cobra Turn. The icing on the cake was a mock combat between the Su-30MK and the Su-35. Viktor G. Pugachov, flying the Su-35, would pull his famous Cobra, causing the two-seater to overshoot. The Su-30MK then rolled right and the fighters would start chasing each other's tails, trying to get into position to fire. Halfway through the turn, Pugachov snapped his fighter up into the Cobra Turn, got a lock-on, and the pursuer was toast. During the Cobra Turn the Su-35 decelerated from 460 km/h (255 kts) to 250 km/h (138 kts), pulling 9 Gs with 90° bank. The aircraft showed no tendency to stall or lose control because of airflow separation. During the Cobra maneuver the aircraft gained some 30 m (98 ft.) of altitude, allowing the pilot to put the nose down to accelerate.

In May/June 1993, Russian and foreign aviation experts had the chance to see the Cobra Turn on the third prototype Su-35 carrying a full load of 12 AAMs. A year later spectators at ILA '94 were treated to the same experience.

The seventh Su-27M (T10M-7, 707 Blue outline) at the NII VVS test centre in Akhtoobinsk, note the low visibility Russian star painted in outline only. (Sergey Sergeyev)

WARBIRD**TECH**
S E R I E S

The ninth prototype, T10M-9 (709 Black outline), was painted in a Middle East version of the splinter camouflage for demonstration in the Middle East and SE Asia. (Yefim Gordon)

The Su-35 has 12 weapons hardpoints versus 10 on the Su-27. (Yefim Gordon)

Two Su-35s in flight. 703 Blue outline carries air-to-ground missiles and smart bombs, while 709 Black outline is armed with AAMs. (Yefim Gordon)

A rare shot of two Su-35s (703 Blue outline and 709 Black outline) taking off from LII's runway. (Yefim Gordon)

The Su-35's takeoff weight has grown slightly, but this has not impaired maneuverability – thanks to the canards. (Yefim Gordon)

Flying the T10M-9, Viktor Pugachov often amazed airshow spectators and aviation experts with his skill and the capabilities of the Su-35. (Yefim Gordon)

Unfortunately, despite the promise it held, the T10-M did not enter service. The Republic of Korea Air Force (ROKAF) expressed an interest in the Su-35 but did not follow up with an order. The Russian Air Force ordered a small batch of Su-27Ms for evaluation purposes. Three production Su-27Ms completed in 1996 (coded *86 Red, 87 Red,* and *88 Red*) were delivered to the 929th GLITs in Akhtoobinsk for trials, where they remain as of this writing. Funding shortages have prevented production of further aircraft.

SU-27 FLANKER

33

This rare shot by the well-known aviation photographer Katsuhiko Tokunaga shows two Su-27Ms during a test flight. The T10M-9 pulls away from the T10M-3 carrying a guided bomb, among other things.

710 Blue *poised for takeoff. Business as usual. (Yefim Gordon)*

One of three production Su-35s on display at the Russian Air Force 929th State Flight Test Centre in Akhtubinsk. (Sergey Sergeyev)

Experimental Thrust-Vectoring Fighter Su-37 (T10M-11) Flanker-E

In the course of its flight tests, the T10-M (Su-35) had performed maneuvers involving high AoAs and airspeeds close to zero. The Pugachov Cobra, Cobra Turn, and tailslide could be used in air-to-air combat; however, active control in these flight modes was virtually impossible because the control surfaces were inefficient at low airspeeds. The pilot could neither control the aircraft's pitch/roll rate nor maintain high alpha, which left him

The 10th Su-27M prototype (T10M-10, 710 Blue) in Zhukovskiy. (Yefim Gordon)

WARBIRDTECH
SERIES

The T10M-11 prototype, 711 White, later re-designated Su-37. This was the first real thrust-vectoring Flanker, delivered to the Sukhoi experimental shop in 1995. (Yefim Gordon)

very little time to get a target lock-on and fire a missile.

Thrust-vectoring control (TVC) was the solution. It was the key to ultra-maneuverability that enabled the fighter to remain in the zero-speed/high-alpha mode for three or four seconds (i.e., long enough to get a lock-on and fire a missile) or quickly recover from this mode.

The Sukhoi OKB began initial TVC studies as early as 1983. The Western press then described two-dimensional vectoring nozzles as the best option; however, General Designer Mikhail P. Simonov insisted on using axisymmetric vectoring nozzles. (Later events showed that he was right. Sukhoi did research on both types of nozzles, but the experimen-

tal 2-D nozzle suffered from severe technological problems.) SibNIA conducted a series of experiments using scale models to test nozzle operation. By 1985 Sukhoi engineers had a clear picture of the forces generated and work began on thrust-vectoring engines. Thus, by the mid 80s the Soviet Union possessed the know-how to create a TVC fighter.

In 1988 and 1990 Sukhoi began a series of tests with the LL-UV (KS) and LL-UV (PS) test-beds. On these aircraft the vectoring nozzle could only move up and down. The results were generally encouraging, and work proceeded on a TVC version of the T10-M.

The first real thrust-vectoring Flanker was the eleventh prototype Su-35 (T10M-11). The new AL-31FU

engine (U = *oopravlyayemoye soplo* – controlled [i.e., movable] nozzle) uprated to 12,800 kgp (28,218 lb st) in full afterburner was selected to power the fighter.

The automatic flight control system governed the vectoring nozzles as well as the control surfaces. It limited G loads automatically to suit the aircraft's all-up weight and flight mode. This was a safety measure to prevent the airframe from being overstressed. As on the Su-35, an automatic spin recovery function was provided; thus, the pilot could concentrate on doing his job without having to worry about G loads and AoAs, or airspeed getting out of hand in the heat of the battle.

The cockpit was equipped with a limited-travel side-stick and included four large color liquid-crystal displays (LCDs) supplied by Sextant Avionique with better backlight protection than cathode-ray tubes (CRTs). The LCDs

Part of the Su-37's avionics was supplied by the French company FPI. The fully interchangeable LCDs came from Sextant Avionique. (Yefim Gordon)

were arranged in T form and comprised a multi-function air data/navigation display, a tactical situation display, a systems status screen, and a weapons/systems selection display.

The mission avionics were also improved. The T10M-11 was to feature an upgraded NIIP N-011M coherent pulse-Doppler fire control radar and the N-012 rear-warning radar. The N-011M was developed for the latest members of the Su-30 series – the Su-37, Su-30MKI, and Su-35UB. The electronic support measures (ESM) suite was upgraded considerably, featuring a new-generation signals intelligence (SIGINT) pack, an infrared intelligence (IRINT) module, a RHAWS, active radar and laser jammers, and chaff/flare dispensers. The communications suite included HF and VHF radios, secure data link, and satellite communications equipment. The new avionics and equipment consumed more electric and hydraulic power, requiring the provision of more powerful generators and pumps.

Painted in a tan/dark earth disruptive camouflage and initially coded *711 Blue*, the T10M-11 made its first flight on 2 April 1996 at the hands of Yevgeniy I. Frolov (Hero of Russia). Igor' V. Votintsev joined the test program soon after. By 14 June Frolov and Votintsev had made 12 flights in the T10M-11 between them. In the spring of 1996 the T10M-11 was unveiled for industry experts and the press in Zhukovskiy. The scenario was repeated – the aircraft received a new official designation, Su-37, because of the major changes to the powerplant and avionics.

Piloted by Yevgeniy Frolov, the Su-37 stole the show at Farnborough International '96. With all control surfaces and the vectoring nozzles moving in concert, the aircraft is capable of pitching up through 180° (wow!) and staying in this tail-first position long enough to fire a missile at a pursuing enemy fighter. This spectacular maneuver has been called the Super Cobra – or, as Frolov calls it, the Stop Cobra.

The Super Cobra logically evolved into a 360° somersault that has become known as the Frolov Chakra. Other maneuvers include a high-speed yo-yo executed in less than ten seconds, a stall turn in a vertical climb, Cobra maneuvers with AoAs of 150 to 180° (with an attitude hold of three or four seconds), a tailslide transforming into a wingover and so on.

In 1997 Sukhoi entered the Su-37 in the exhibit list of the 42nd Paris Air Show at Le Bourget. The aircraft arrived in Paris on 19 June, the closing day, wearing the exhibit code 344. Many of the industry delegations at Le Bourget delayed their departure just to have a look at the Su-37. However, the flight display was marred by an incident. The first three demo flights went OK, but on the fourth flight the landing gear would not retract. Frolov did a Cobra and landed hastily, cutting the flight short. It turned out that someone had

The Su-37 is powered by modified AL-31FU engines with thrust vectoring in the pitch plane. The overlapping petals are clearly visible. (Yefim Gordon Archive)

The Su-37 takes off from Kubinka during the 16th VA's 50-year jubilee show on 8 August 1997, still bearing its Paris show number from the previous June. (Yefim Gordon)

Yevgeni Frolov makes a tight turn in the stores free cleaned up Su-37. (Yefim Gordon)

moved the emergency extension handle, disabling gear retraction. A little thing like this was of course fixed immediately, and *711 White* performed another display routine flawlessly. At the IDEX '97 trade fair in Dubai and the FIDAE '98 airshow in Santiago de Chile (the latter event started on 23 March 1998), the fighter was somewhat surprisingly demonstrated under a new designation, Su-37MR; no one seems to know what the R stands for!

Test and demo flights have demonstrated the AL-31FP's excellent resistance to surge, even when the aircraft literally travels tail first. The AL-31FP's axisymmetric nozzle is attached to an annular frame powered by two pairs of hydraulic rams, tilting vertically through ±15°. The frame is made of steel on prototype engines, but titanium is used on production engines to save weight. Also, the nozzle tilting mechanism is hydraulically actuated on prototype engines but is powered by the fuel system on production engines to improve survivability. Sealing the casing/nozzle joint effectively was perhaps the biggest challenge, since seepage of exhaust gases with a temperature around 2,000° C (3,632° F) and a pressure around 15 kg/cm² (214 psi) was guaranteed to cause a fire. Another major task solved by the engineers was complete nozzle control automation, as the pilot should not have to work separate TVC levers or switches. The nozzle is controlled by digital computers forming part of the FBW control system; the pilot simply works the stick and pedals, and the computers take care of the rest. Another ingenious feature of the AL-31FP is the mono-crystalline turbine blades designed for very high loads.

A second Su-37, reportedly converted from T10M-12, first flew in mid 1998 and was initially powered by AL-31F; installation of thrust-vectoring AL-37FPs was expected in late 1998. The status of this aircraft, if still extant, remains unclear. At present the Su-37's trials program has virtually ground to a halt – mainly due to lack of customer interest in single-seaters. Foreign customers for the Su-30 series – primarily the Indian Air Force and the Chinese People's Liberation Army Air Force (PLAAF) – prefer the two-seat Su-30MK that comes in customized versions, the Su-30MKI (with TVC and canards), and the Su-30MKK (without TVC and canards), respectively.

Multi-Role Export Fighter Su-27SK & SMK Flanker-B

From the outset, the Su-27 had considerable export potential. Still, for various reasons – mainly political ones – exports of new Flankers were limited to India, China and Vietnam.

The export version of the Su-27 (T10-S) for China and Vietnam was designated Su-27SK. S means *sereeynyy* (production, used attributively) while K stands for *kommehrcheskiy* (commercial, ie, downgraded customer version). The first Chinese-assembled air-

The Su-27SMK demonstrator at KnAAPO airfield with its version presented on the nose with the production code. (KnAAPO)

craft was flight tested in December 1998. It differed from Soviet Air Force Flanker-*Bs* in having a reinforced landing gear, a MTOW increased to 33,000 kg (72,751 lbs.) and slightly downgraded avionics, with foreign avionics as a customer option.

A more capable version, designated Su-27SMK, was developed as a cheaper alternative to the Su-35/Su-37, the M standing for *modernizeerovannyy* (upgraded). Changes as compared to the Su-27SK include two extra hardpoints and an improved targeting, navigation, communications and ECM suite. Two of the pylons are wet, permitting the carriage of 2,000-litre (440 Imperial gallon) drop tanks, and a retractable IFR probe is provided. The Su-27SMK features an improved version of the N-001 pulse-Doppler fire control radar with better air-to-air and air-to-ground capability and can carry up to six KAB-500KR TV-guided smart bombs. Western avionics and/or weapons may be integrated at customer request.

Multi-role export fighter Su-27KI (Su-30KI)

Another upgrade to the Flanker-B was developed by Sukhoi and KnAAPO for the Indonesian Air Force. In the popular press this aircraft has also been referred to as the Su-30KI (despite being single-seat), the Su-27KI (the I obviously standing for Indonesia), and simply as a modified Su-27SK.

The uncoded prototype made its first flight on 28th June 1998 at the hands of KnAAPO test pilot Yevgeniy Revoonov. Outwardly the Su-27KI differs from the standard Su-27 Flanker-B only in having a retractable refueling probe on the port side of the nose. Other changes to the equipment included an upgraded N-001M radar capable of working with R-77 (RVV-AE) missiles, the addition of a global posi-

tioning system (GPS), a Western-standard automatic approach and instrument landing system (ILS/VOR).

In December 1999 the aircraft took part in the LIMA '99 airshow held at Langkawi AB, Kuala Lumpur. A few months later it was on show at the DSA'2000 industry-only defense fair held in Kuala Lumpur on 11th-14th April 2000. Negotiations with Indonesia on the purchase dragged on for years – and came to nothing. This was probably just as well – the deal would have been politically damaging for Russia, since Indonesia was then subjected to international ostracism because of the hostilities in East Timor.

Multi-Role Fighter Su-27SM

Russian Air Forces upgrade. First conversion of Su-27S for Russian Air Forces flew at Komsomolsk on 27 December 2002; upgrade adds two MFI-9 178 x 127 mm (7 x 5 in.) LCDs, satellite navigation and new radar computer. Second stage upgrade planned for 2005, adding L175 Khibiny EW system, quiet

One of the first upgraded Su-27SM during the tests in Zhukovskiy carrying AAMs on the wing tip rails. (Viktor Drushlyakov)

radar and electro-optic targeting pod. First-stage upgrades were completed with 12 aircraft now in service. The multi-Role Export Fighter Su-27SKM export version of Su-27SM.

Two-Seat Multi-Role Fighters

Operational experience with single-seat interceptors (including the Flanker-B) showed that in a modern dogfight the workload was simply too high for a single pilot, who had to fly the jet and operate the weapons control system while experiencing high G loads. A second crewmember was clearly needed to reduce pilot workload. Besides, providing dual-flight controls enabled the crew to operate more efficiently during long sorties. One pilot would fly the aircraft, control the weapons, and take care of close-in fighting, while the other would be the weapons systems operator (WSO),

detecting and destroying the enemy at long range. This led to the development of a whole range of new two-seat tactical aircraft based on the Su-27UB.

Multi-Role Fighter Trainer Su-27UBM

Russian Air Forces upgrade. The first modified Su-27UB was delivered from Irkutsk plant to LII at Zhukovsky 6 March 2001. The further seven conversions were planned to take place before end of same year; two were completed by September 2001. New equipment included GPS and three 152 x 203 mm (6 x 8 in.) MFDs.

Interceptor Su-30 (Su-27PU, T10-PU, *izdeliye* 10-4PU)

Cuts in the Soviet Air Force's fighter fleet, the sheer length of the Soviet Union's northern borders, and

The Su-27SKM 305 Black prototype. Modelers will note the serial appearing on the inside face of the tailfin. (Sukhoi OKB)

The Su-27SKM prototype during a test flight displaying an assortment of stores on both wing and fuselage hardpoints. (Sukhoi OKB)

The Su-30KI taxies out for a demonstration flight on 19 August 1999 during the MAKS-99 airshow in Zhukovskiy. Another version, another color scheme. (Yefim Gordon)

The Su-30KI elegantly displays its upper surface as it makes a turn during a demo flight at MAKS-99 with nozzles set straight but tapered. (Yefim Gordon)

Seen here in Zhukovskiy on 6 March 2001, the first Su-27UB upgraded to Su-27UBM standard for the Russian Air Force. (Yefim Gordon Archive)

The first Su-27UBM prototype on LII's runway in Zhukovskiy. The rear cockpit view can be appreciated from this angle. (Yefim Gordon Archive)

the scarcity of airbases in the northern regions of the country prompted the Sukhoi OKB to develop Su-27UB trainer into a specialized two-seat interceptor. This aircraft could operate as a tactical airborne command post, the WSO giving directions to other aircraft during concerted action. To this end a tactical situation display in the rear cockpit and in-flight refueling became essential.

Work on a two-seat inter-cep-tor/ABCP version of the Su-27 began in the mid 1980s. The Su-27UB, with its large internal fuel volume and heavy armament, was chosen as the starting point. A group of Sukhoi OKB engineers converted two standard Su-27UBs at IAPO in the summer and autumn of 1988. Coded *05 Blue* and *06 Blue*, the proof-of-concept aircraft were designated T10PU-5 and T10PU-6, respectively, and bore the IAPO in-house designation *izdeliye* 10-4PU; The PU suffix is sometimes deciphered as (*vozdoosh-nyy*) *poonkt oopravlen*iya – airborne command post, but this is a statement open to doubt; *perekhvaht*chik *oosovershen*stvovannyy – interceptor, improved, appears more likely. New features included a retractable refueling probe, new navigation suite, and changes to the FBW controls, life support, and weapons systems. The aircraft passed its trials program with flying colors and was cleared for production at IAPO as the Su-30.

On 14 April 1992 the first production Su-30 took off with Boolanov and Maksimenkov at the controls.

Two views of the first prototype Su-30 (T10PU-5). Although there were no aerodynamic changes, the refueling capability, FBW and WCS improvements were a significant upgrade. (Sukhoi OKB archive)

The T10PU-5 in Akhtoobinsk during NII VVS tests that commenced in 1988 leading to final production in Irkutsk. (Yefim Gordon)

Two production Su-30s at Savasleika AFB. This is typical of a Soviet style operational ramp with portable blast deflectors, "streetlamps" and small shelters for the harsh winter weather. (Yefim Gordon Archive)

Pilot's instrument panel of the T10PU-5. The lower leg enclosures no doubt prevent damage from the instrument panel in case of ejection. (Yefim Gordon)

the Su-30s gave their first public performance at MosAeroShow '92 and have since become regulars at various airshows. Most of the production Su-30s are operated by the IA PVO's 148th Operational Conversion Unit (TsBPiPLS – *Tsentr boyevoy podgotovki i pereoochivaniya lyotnovo sostahva*, Combat and Conversion Training Centre) at Savostleyka AB near Nizhniy Novgorod.

Interceptor Su-30K (izdeliye 10-4PK)

This is an export version of the Su-30 and differs only slightly from Russian Air Force examples in identification friend-or-foe (IFF), navigation, and communications equipment.

On 20 April 1994 a Russian-Indian working group convened in New Delhi to discuss cooperation in aerospace matters. One of the items was possible license production of the Su-30MK by Hindustan Aeronautics Ltd. (HAL) that had a history of building Soviet fighters. On 30 November 1996, after more than two years of negotiations, a contract was signed for the delivery of 40 Su-30K/MKs to the Indian Air Force.

Unlike the single-seat Su-27, the Su-30 was not merely an air superiority fighter. Its missions included long-range combat air patrol (CAP) and escort duties, AEW&C, and pilot training. While being capable of performing the same tasks as the Su-27UB, the new aircraft had a much greater combat radius and endurance and could operate more effectively in a group of fighters by virtue of its command post function.

The Su-30 retains the excellent agility of the other members of the Flanker family. New air-to-air weapons have greatly increased its combat potential. On internal fuel only (9,400 kg/20,723 lbs.) it has a range of 3,600 km (2,000 nm). With aerial refueling, range and endurance is limited only by how much the crew can take, although a ten-hour mission time limit has been set by medical specialists.

Unfortunately, the collapse of the Soviet Union caused Su-30 production to slow. The very few production aircraft built to date are in service with the PVO. A notable exception is the first two production Su-30s that were delivered to Anatoliy N. Kvochur's *Ispytahteli* (test pilots) display team at LII after completing their trials program. They are sometimes referred to as Su-27PUs by the popular press – a designation that never existed. Painted in a striking blue/red/white color scheme and coded *596* and *597 White*,

A modified Su-27PU piloted by Anatoliy Kvochur. The ease of connection to the Il-78 Midas tanker is obvious; note the Singapore Airlines badge showing their co-operation with the Russian Test Center. (Yefim Gordon archive)

A Su-30K near the Sukhoi hangar in Zhukovskiy. This example flew unrefueled across the Atlantic in 1994 en route to the FIDAE exhibition in Chile. (Yefim Gordon)

This Su-30K, 603 Black outline, was painted in desert camouflage for demonstration in the Middle East and South East Asian states. (Yefim Gordon)

Sukhoi test pilot Igor' Votintsev taking off in the Su-30K. The undercarriage retraction normally commences immediately on becoming airborne. (Yefim Gordon)

IAF pilots and ground crews took conversion training with Sukhoi in Zhukovskiy in January-April 1997, with Pugachov acting as instructor pilot. On 11 June the IAF held an official ceremony at Lohegaon AB to mark the service entry of the Su-30K and the first eight aircraft were declared fully operational with the 24 Sqn.

On 22 March 1998 three Su-30Ks participated in the Vayu Shakti '98

WARBIRD**TECH**
S E R I E S

The Su-30K lands in Zhukovskiy. The drag chute deploys from the tail cone above and between the engine nozzles. (Yefim Gordon)

The Su-30MKI prototype (56 Blue) during trials in July 1997. The main gear well is easily seen here, allowing a thin wing without too adversely affecting the fuselage cross section. (Aviapanorama)

exercise in Pokhran, Rajasthan. The fighters demolished 11 targets, including a mock runway, with pinpoint bomb strikes. Then, by dogfighting with a MiG-29 Fulcrum after a spectacular display of aerobatics, it stunned the audience that included 25 foreign military attaches.

Multi-Role Fighter Su-30MK (izdeliye 10-4PMK)

The Su-30 was primarily designed for the IA PVO, which could use its capabilities as a long-range patrol fighter and interceptor to the full. However, new precision air-to-surface missiles (including anti-shipping missiles) became available to the VVS and the naval air arm (AVMF – *Aviahtsiya voyenno-morskovo flota*) in the early '90s. The aircraft was converted from the first production Su-30 previously operated by the *Ispytahteli* display team. It received a disruptive sand/brown desert camouflage and a new low-visibility tactical code, *603 Black*.

Precision weapons enhance the Su-30MK's capabilities; for instance, the Kh-59M can transmit a "bomb's eye view" (the picture seen by its TV guidance system) to the WSO's display at a distance in excess of 100 km (55 nm). Having located the target, the WSO can guide the missile manually all the way in and score a direct hit. The weapons control system was to feature a new-generation coherent pulse-Doppler radar with a 1m (3 ft. 3.37 in.) scanner. It was to track ten aerial targets at up to 100 km (55 nm), guiding missiles to two priority threats at up to 65 km (36 nm). The WCS was to automatically download target data to the missiles and fire them at preset intervals and in a preset sequence. The

Sukhoi test pilot Igor' Votintsev and Su-30K 603 Black outline. The offset IRST ball and refueling probe are clearly seen. (Yefim Gordon airchive)

Two more views of the first Su-30MKI prototype. Note the independent rear access steps and bridging piece to protect the control surface from accidental damage. The vectoring nozzles are also apparent in this photo. (Yefim Gordon)

The ill-starred first prototype Su-30MKI, 01 Blue, on LII's runway. Previously 56 Blue, its first official appearance was on 15 June 1998. (Yefim Gordon)

pilots were to use helmet-mounted sights; target data would also be presented on the direct vision display and HUD. The aircraft was also equipped with an IRST unit with day/night channels and a laser ranger. Western avionics and/or weapons would be integrated at customer request. Both cockpits feature identical sets of flight and weapons controls, enabling either of the two crewmen to fly the aircraft or use the weapons. On-station time during CAP missions is 10 hours.

The Su-30MK was displayed again at IDEX '93 in Dubai and was one of the highlights of the FIDAE '94 airshow in Santiago de Chile, flying the Atlantic Ocean on internal fuel only – a sensation in itself.

That year it was demonstrated at ILA '94 (at Berlin-Schonefeld) and Farnborough International '94. On the latter occasion the Su-30MK put on such an impressive aerobatics display with a full load of bombs and rockets that competitors had to admit no Western aircraft could match it. The aircraft was also present at MAKS '93 and MAKS '95 in Zhukovskiy, as well as airshows in China, Malaysia, and India.

Still, the Su-30MK remains in prototype form as of this writing, even though IAPO has had a complete set of manufacturing drawings and documents for several years. It is expected to be designated Su-30MKR if produced (at Irkutsk) for Russian Air Forces.

Multi-Role Fighter Su-30MKI (Su-30MK/Indian version, izdeliye 10-4PMK-2) Flanker-H

Initial deliveries under the Indian contract were Su-30Ks differing from Russian AF Su-30s only slightly in avionics fit. Starting in the year 2000, however, IAPO and Sukhoi were to upgrade the Su-30K to improve its agility, performance, and firepower, effectively a next-generation aircraft. New features included automatically controlled canards *a la* Su-27M (Su-35) for better low-speed/high-alpha handling, AL-31FP engines with axisymmetric thrust-vectoring nozzles for ultra-maneuverability, and a completely new mission avionics suite giving the fighter counter-air, air-to-ground, and maritime strike capability.

Close-up to the Su-30MKI's vectoring nozzles. Computer control allows the nozzles to aid taxiing as well as in flight maneuvers. (Yefim Gordon)

The fighter received the designation Su-30MKI (*indeeyskiy* – Indian) or *izdeliye* 10-4PMK-2 to distinguish it from the original Su-30MK lacking canards and TVC. The Su-30Ks delivered initially would be updated to Su-30MKI standard in due time. The avionics suite included a new multimode fire control radar, capable of tracking 15 aerial targets while guiding missiles to four priority threats and having high resistance to ground clutter. The Su-30MKI also featured a new cockpit indication system with high-resolution liquid-crystal color MFDs, plus an entirely new flight data recorder (FDR) that, apart from its primary function, recorded tactical information as well.

The T10PMK-1 was originally powered by 12,800 kgp (28,218 lb st) AL-31FU engines with pitch/yaw thrust vectoring, but these went unserviceable during early flight tests. Less powerful AL-31FPs with pitch-only thrust vectoring (±15°) had to be fitted as a stopgap. Unlike the Su-37, however, the TVC nozzle hinges were tilted 32° outward from the horizontal and generated a side force when deflected differentially, improving the fighter's agility and control response at near-zero speeds. The nozzle petal actuators were powered by the fuel system, not hydraulically.

The Su-30MKI was shown publicly for the first time on 16 August 1998, when *01 Blue* participated in the annual Aviation Day flypast at Moscow's Tushino airfield. In November 1998 the type had its international debut when it was displayed at the Aero India '98 airshow in Bangalore.

In June 1999 the first prototype arrived in Le Bourget where it was to participate in the 43rd Paris Air Show.

05 Blue, the first pre-production Su-30MK, inside Sukhoi's hangar at LII, Zhukovskiy. (Yefim Gordon)

05 Blue, *the first pre-production Su-30MK, following modifications and repaint, seen on LII's runway with the nozzles tapered and chute cover open after landing. (Yefim Gordon)*

and exploded – an eerie replay of Anatoliy Kvochur's accident in a MiG-29 Fulcrum-A at the 1989 show. The crew was rushed to a hospital, but released the following day. Neither Aver'yanov nor Shendrik suffered any injuries. The accident report was never published, but aviation experts agreed the cause was pilot error.

For the Indian contract, HAL was granted a license to build 140 Su-30MKIs (since reduced to 120) with license production at the Nasik division to be in four stages. The first aircraft assembled from Russian-supplied components flew in 2004, with two more following before the end of the year. Six were completed in 2005 and another eight in 2006. After that, production proceeds at 10 per year. At this stage the

The first prototype Su-30MKI takes off from Zhukovski. Note how far back the second pilot/WCO sits, giving very little rearward view. (Yefim Gordon)

The first prototype Su-30MKI toting its maximum ordnance load in strike configuration: 32 250-kg FAB-250 bombs on MBD3-u6-68 multiple ejector racks and two R-73 AAMs on the wingtip pylons (Sukhoi OKB)

Unfortunately, on 12 June it crashed during a training flight prior to the grand opening. While demonstrating a controlled spin that was part of the display program, Aver'yanov recovered too late, making one turn too many. As it pulled out of the dive, the fighter struck the ground taildown. It climbed away, but with the starboard jetpipe broken by the impact and flames belching from the port engine due to a ruptured fuel line. The damaged starboard engine nozzle was pointing about 30° up (twice its design limit), causing an uncontrollable pitch-up. As the Su-30MKI stood on its tail and the nose started falling, pilots Aver'yanov and Shendrik ejected. Seconds later the fighter pancaked beside the runway aircraft are made of locally manufactured items; the airframe built by the Nasik factory, the engines in Koraput, the radar and other electronics in Hyderabad, the flight avionics in Korv, and the hydraulic and pneumatic components in Laknau. To facilitate product support, Sukhoi and HAL established a customs warehouse that enables spares to be delivered to the IAF within two or

This dramatic shot depicts the last moments of the Su-30MKI 01 Blue as it crashes at Le Bourget on June 12, 1999. (Helmut Walther)

The second Su-30MKI prototype on the ground and in flight. (Yefim Gordon)

three days. The U.S. $3.3 billion licensing agreement provides for further upgrades, but not before actual license production has started.

Multi-Role Fighter Su-30MKK (Su-30MK/Chinese version) Flanker-G

The Su-30MKI started a new trend. Like their British and American colleagues, Russian combat aircraft designers are now creating new versions to suit the needs of each specific customer. The next spin-off was developed for the PLAAF of China, hence the designation Su-30MKK (the second K stands for *kitayskiy* – Chinese).

The Su-30MKK differs from the Indian version both structurally and in equipment, incorporating some features of the Su-35. It lacks the canards and TVC feature of the Su-30MKI, being powered by standard AL-31Fs. On the other hand, it has the tall, thick, square-tipped CFRP fins of the Su-35 incorporating fuel tanks.

The Su-30MKK prototype was converted from the very first Su-30 (T10PU-5, *05 Blue*) in early 1999, making its maiden flight at LII on 9 March. It was decided to build the Su-30MKK at KnAAPO, which until now has produced only single-seat versions of the Flanker (apart from a few initial-production Su-27UBs), instead of IAPO that traditionally builds the two-seaters. Geographical proximity to China, the customer, may have been a factor. On the other hand, the Chinese Su-27UBKs had been built in Irkutsk and there was no real reason why the Su-30MKK should not be manufactured there as well.

Coded *501 Blue* and painted in a three-tone grey/bluish grey camouflage, the first pre-production aircraft took to the air in Komsomol'sk-on-Amur on 19 May 1999 at the hands of project test pilot Vyacheslav Aver'yanov. The second pre-production aircraft (*502 Blue*) was completed

Close-up of the Su-30MKI's canards. Note Lyul'ka-Saturn emblem on the air intakes consisting of the stylized Cyrilic letters "AL" for Arkhip Lyul'ka. (Yefim Gordon)

The second Su-30MKI prototype shortly after a demonstration flight at Zhukovskiy, the masts are flagpoles being prepared for the airshow. (Yefim Gordon)

Two views of the first pre-production Su-30MK in IAPO's assembly shop. The stand prevents the CG shift from part removal causing the aircraft to tip. (Yefim Gordon)

in mid-summer in a PLAAF-style slate grey color scheme. The third and fourth Su-30MKKs (*503 Black* and *504 Black*) were test flown in a primer finish; the former aircraft later received the same grey color scheme, becoming *503 Blue*. The first batch of 10 production Su-30MKKs was reportedly delivered in late 2000. Interestingly, almost simultaneously the PLAAF took delivery of four Su-27UBKs built by IAPO.

Chinese production of the Flanker switched to the Su-30MKK after 80 aircraft. However, China reportedly ordered 45 KnAAPO-built Su-30MKKs and placed a supplementary order (initially quoted as 24, but later stated to be 40) in June 2001. The first batch of 10 Su-30MKKs were delivered to China on 20 December 2000; nine followed in March/April 2001, and 10 more on 21 August. Early Su-30MKKs variously reported with Three Swords Air Regiment at Yuxikou, near Nanjing or at Wuhu, Anhui.

Multi-Fole Fighter Su-30MKM

On 22 January 2001 the *Utusan Malaysia* daily reported that the Royal Malaysian Air Force (RMAF, or TUDM – *Tentera Udara Diraja Malaysia*) was in the final stages of closing a deal for the delivery of Su-30MKM fighters. A U.S. $900 million contract was initialed 19 May 2003.

The first prototype Su-30 (T10PU-5) following conversion as the Su-30MKK demonstrator, the starboard outer stores pylon has been removed for this flight. (Viktor Drushlyakov)

501 Blue, the first real prototype Su-30MKK, seen during a test flight. Note the dielectric panels on the stabilator tips and the weapons mounted on the center stations, between the nacelles. (Viktor Drushlyakov)

501 Blue with one of the standard weapons fits: two Kh-31P ARMs, two Kh-59M AGMs, two R-73 short range AAMs, and two R-77 (RVV-AE) medium-range AAMs. (Sukhoi OKB)

An Indian Air Force Su-30MKI seen at the Aero India airshow at Bangalore in southern India. (IAPO)

The Su-30MKK features taller, increased-area CFRP fins with integral tanks a la Su-35. Note the "brandy stripes" on the fins of this one and just how far forward of the stabilators lie the twin fins. (Sukhoi OKB)

Multi-Role Fighter Su-35UB

The Su-30MK (Su-30MKI, Su-30MKK) was not the last in the Su-30 series line of fighters. KnAAPO has succeeded in developing a new two-seat multi-role version of the Flanker – the Su-35UB – on its own. The aircraft was designed to combine the Su-37's strong points with the best features of both the Su-30MKI and the MKK. Interestingly, for the first time KnAAPO engineers made large-scale use of computer-aided design (CAD) when designing the aircraft.

Of all Su-30 versions developed as of this writing, the Su-35UB has the most sophisticated avionics suite. It is equipped with an N-011M fire control radar compatible with the entire range of AAMs, ASMs, and bombs. The Su-35UB prototype was completed in mid 2000. Coded *801 Blue* and wearing a bright blue/light blue/black camouflage, this aircraft was powered by AL-31F engines on its first flight, lacking TVC capability (the intended engines were apparently unavailable at the time). Flight tests began in the autumn of 2000.

Multi-Role Fighter Su-30K2

In 1996 the Sukhoi OKB started work on another two-seat multi-role fighter designated Su-30K2. It differs from the basic Su-30 in having a new wide forward fuselage with side-by-side seating.

The Su-30KN makes a demonstration flight at the MAKS-99 airshow in Zhukovskiy. With the underslung bombs, there must be a negative effect on speed and agility. (Yefim Gordon)

MAKS '99 was the first time a natural metal aircraft was put on display in Zhukovskiy. The range of materials used is very obvious in this image. (Yefim Gordon)

The Su-30KN makes a formation take-off with the Su-27PD (598 White). (Yefim Gordon)

WARBIRDTECH
S E R I E S

Close-up of the weapons carried on the pylons of the Su-30KN. The arrays seen at airshows sometimes make little sense operationally. (Yefim Gordon)

Front view of the Su-30KN. The rear pilot/WCO has a reasonable view over the front seat and cockpit frame. (Yefim Gordon)

Multi-Role Fighter Su-30KN

The collapse of the Soviet Union triggered a lengthy economic crisis. Defense spending was cut dramatically. Ordering such expensive aircraft as the Su-35/Su-37 and Su-30MK was impossible in these conditions. Meanwhile, the Flankers already in service were growing obsolete. In February 1999 IAPO offered a low-cost mid-life update (MLU) program for Russian Su-30s as a private venture. No separate designation existed

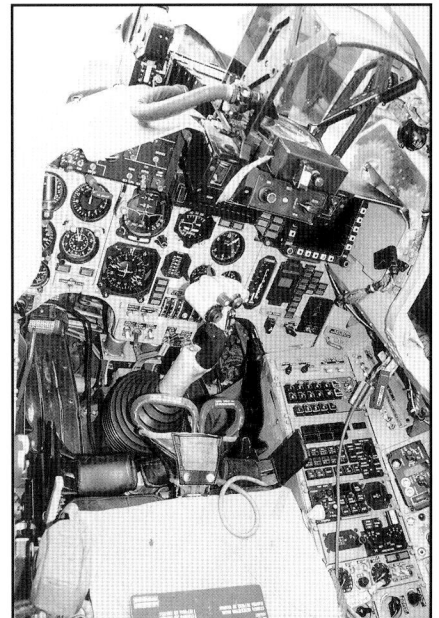

The front cockpit of the same aircraft; note the very prominent HUD. (Yefim Gordon)

Footage of the Su-30KN launching an R-77 (RVV-AE) AAM and dropping a TV-guided bomb. (Yefim Gordon)

at first, but from 2000 onwards the aircraft is known as the Su-30KN.

In both cockpits the standard cathode-ray tube (CRT) direct vision display has been replaced by a 5 x 5 in. MFI-55 (*mnogofoonktseeonahl'nyy indikahtor*) color liquid-crystal MFD. This displays flight or tactical information and is easier to adapt to, enabling service pilots to quickly master the precision weapons. The new equipment increased empty weight by a mere 30 kg (66 lbs.), so the fighter's performance is virtually unaffected. The combat potential is increased several times, enabling the Su-30KN to rival the USA's Boeing (McDD) F-15E Strike Eagle.

A standard production Su-30 was set aside as the future Su-30KN prototype, making its first flight in March 1999. By April the fighter arrived in Zhukovskiy to undergo manufacturer's flight tests. Coded *302 Blue*, the still-unpainted (and nameless) aircraft was displayed at MAKS-99. Wearing recently applied grey/black/white "splatter" camouflage, the Su-30KN prototype took part in the Hydro Aviation Show held in Ghelendzhik in September 2000. The aircraft arrived from Akhtoobinsk where it was then undergoing Stage II of the state acceptance trials matching the avionics suite to the MiG-29SMT.

Fyodorov and Korzhooyev regard the Su-30KN mid-life update as the best upgrade option for the Russian Air Force in the current conditions because it does not require extensive and costly changes to the avionics suite.

Some industry experts claim that existing versions of the Flanker family have inadequate air-to-surface capability. Hence NPO Mashinostroyeniya is integrating the Alpha anti-shipping missile with the Su-30KN's weapons control system. Outside the CIS, the Su-27 and Su-30 are operated mainly by India, mainland China, and Vietnam, all of them marine powers which urgently need aircraft with enhanced anti-ship capabilities.

Multi-Role Fighter Su-30KNM

The program began in 2002. Modifications involve larger (152 x 203 mm; 6 x 8 in.), MFI-68 screens (three for pilot and four for WSO), A Pero (Feather) phased-array radar and equivalent of MIL-STD-1553B databus. An upgrade of air force aircraft may begin in 2005.

ALL ABOARD!

Shipboard Fighter Prototypes Su-27K (T10-K)

Initial research and feasibility studies for a conventional takeoff and landing (CTOL) aircraft carrier started in 1968. Soviet (Russian) carriers were, and still are, referred to as "heavy aircraft-carrying cruisers." The term avoided an international treaty prohibiting the passage of aircraft carriers through the straits of the Bosphorus and Dardanelles. As the program got underway, the aircraft designers were immediately faced with the task of selecting the best takeoff mode – deck catapult or ski jump.

Catapult-launched aircraft are fitted with a so-called jump strut to increase AOA – a nose gear unit with an oleo extended to its full length. This requires the forward fuselage to be reinforced, incurring a weight penalty and impairing performance. A high launch speed is required because the aircraft's AOA on deck is close to zero and the trajectory is almost horizontal. Since the catapult track is only about 90 m (295 ft.) long, the acceleration to 300 km/h is a violent experience. During launch the pilot is subjected to 4.5 Gs, which often causes G-loc (G-induced loss of consciousness).

Conversely, on a carrier with a ski jump the aircraft is restrained by pop-up detents, allowing it to go to full afterburner before release. After leaving the ski jump the aircraft has a positive AOA and pitch angular speed. These increase as the aircraft accelerates, assisting climb. Thus, the pilot stays in control at all times, which enhances flight safety. The ski jump clearance speed (120-140 km/h or 66-77 kts) is approximately half that of a

The T10-25 testbed equipped with an arrestor hook. This aircraft made numerous ski-jump takeoffs and arrestor wire engagements at the test facility at Novofyodorovka AB in Saki. (Sukhoi OKB archive)

The T10-20KTM, a full-scale mockup of the T10-K based on the initial production Su-27, used for hangar compatibility tests. Note the single nosewheel, the very basic wing hinge, and the absence of canards and refueling probe. (Sukhoi OKB archive)

catapult launch, which means stringent requirements apply to aircraft stability and controllability.

After carefully studying the catapult and ski jump options and analyzing operational experience with shipboard fighters abroad, the Sukhoi and Mikoyan bureaus decided on the ski jump.

By mid 1982, the RDTC at Novofyodorovka AB in Saki, Crimea, was fully operational. The official appellation NIUTK (*Naoochno-issledovatel'skiy i oochebno-trenirovochnyy kompleks* – RDTC) soon gave way to the easily pronouncible nickname "Nitka" (Thread) which soon found its way into official documents. The complex comprised the T-1 ski jump, a rather provisional deck catapult, and two arrestor systems (one cable, one chain).

The shipboard fighter was conceived as a multi-role aircraft. Apart from air defense, it was to act as a "hunter," destroying enemy ASW, transport and AWACS aircraft, make anti-shipping strikes, supporting marine landings, escorting land-based aircraft, setting minefields, and reconnaissance.

Sukhoi and Mikoyan began ski jump research in 1982. A ski jump and an arrestor wire system were added to the runway at Novofyodorovka AB. Several development aircraft, including the third prototype Su-27 (T10-3), were used for carrier operations research. Company test pilot Nikolay F. Sadovnikov made the first takeoffs from the T-1 ski jump same year (T = *tramplin* – ski jump).

The next year the T10-3 was retrofitted with an arrestor hook; so was T10-25, a production-standard Su-27. The original T-1 ski jump proved unsuitable, so the two converted aircraft were used for landing trials while a reprofiled T-2 ski jump was under construction. Nikolay Sadovnikov and Viktor G. Pugachov (LII) made

The first prototype of the naval Flanker, T10K-1 (37 Blue), was a converted "landlubber" airframe with no provision for wing and stabilator folding. Sukhoi test pilot Nikolay Sadovnikov is flying the aircraft in these photos. (Sukhoi OKB archive)

The T10K-1 takes on fuel from the Aircraft 02-10 testbed fitted with an UPAZ-1A "buddy" refueling pack. (Sukhoi OKB archive)

The third prototype, T10K-3, was the only one to lack a tactical code; logically, it should have been 49 Blue. (Yefim Gordon)

The fourth prototype, T10K-4 (59 Blue), made numerous landings on SNS Tbilisi along with the other prototypes. (Sukhoi OKB archive)

more than 100 ski jump takeoffs and arrestor wire engagements in 1982-84, proving that fourth-generation fighters could operate from a carrier without a steam catapult.

Full-scale development of the navalized Flanker began in 1984 under the designation T10-K; the official designation Su-27K was assigned later. Mikhail P. Simonov supervised the T10-K program; however, the actual design effort was led by Konstantin Marbashev, who should thus be regarded as the chief project engineer.

The T10-K introduced new features. Small one-piece canard foreplanes were installed just aft of the cockpit, requiring the LERXes to be slightly reshaped. Wing area was increased, but the span remained unchanged. The large flaperons gave way to two-section flaps, with ailerons outboard replacing the rigid trailing edge. The powerful TE flaps increased lift 1.5 times, markedly reducing approach speed. The LE flaps were deflected automatically.

The wings had power folding, as did the stabilators – a unique feature among carrier-borne aircraft. The vertical tails were shortened slightly for hangar access. The tail "stinger" was shortened and reprofiled. The tip of the tail stinger and the radome hinged upwards.

The navigation and communications suite included special equipment for carrier operations. The brake parachute was deleted and its container replaced by an L-006 (SPO-15) "Beryoza" RHAWS (the RHAWS antennas were moved to the tail stinger). The IRST "ball" was offset to starboard to improve downward visibility. The wing folding hinges reduced wing tank volume, so a retractable L-shaped refueling probe, offset to port, was fitted ahead of the windscreen.

The landing gear was strengthened for no-flare landings. The single-nose wheel and levered suspension were replaced by twin wheels and an increased-stroke oleo. The main wheels now had heavy-duty increased-pressure tires more resistant to wear and tear, permitting higher gross-weight takeoffs. The main wheel oleos incorporated tiedown shackles. The K-36DM ejection seat was inclined 30° aft. Finally, the whole airframe was reinforced and resistant materials were used to protect the airframe and powerplant against the corrosive ocean environment.

The PNK-10K control and navigation suite included an autopilot linked to an autothrottle and enabled automatic route following with navigational inputs from LORAN and satellite navigation (GPS) systems, as well as automatic carrier approach directed by the "Resistor-K42" landing aid. The latter enabled ICAO Cat II automatic approach and landing. The avionics that went with the "resistor" autoland system were put through their paces on the "02-10"

refueling systems testbed (T10U-2), which thus became an avionics testbed. An active beacon was attached to the nose-gear unit to provide a better radar signature. All avionics were virtually jam-proof, essential when operating in the intense electromagnetic environment on a carrier.

Besides the GSh-301 30-mm gun and up to 10 AAMs, the T10-K's armament included the 3M80 "Moskit" (Mosquito) supersonic anti-shipping missile. The naval Flanker had 12 hardpoints instead of 10, and the ordnance load was limited to 6,500 kg (14,329 lbs.) – just 500 kg (1,102 lbs.) above that of the land-based version – because of the fighter's high MTOW.

The Su-27 could take off easily with a full fuel and weapons load, using only 105 m (344 ft.). The ski jump was set at 15° and the normal glideslope angle was 4°. Landing was possible in automatic, directed (com-

The fifth prototype, T10K-5 (69 Blue), was in the static park at MosAeroShow '92 in Zhukovskiy. (Yefim Gordon)

A top view of the T10K-7 with a standard complement of AAMs. (Military Technology)

79 Blue *in the demonstration hangar at Kubinka AB. (Yefim Gordon)*

For air defense missions, the Su-27K is usually armed with R-27 medium-range AAMs and R-73 short-range AAMs. (Yefim Gordon)

The Su-27K's folding wings, stabilizers, and pitot boom make the aircraft more compact for hangar stowage. (Yefim Gordon)

mand link), and manual mode. To this end the carrier was equipped with VOR/localizer and glideslope beacons, approach radar, and a "Luna-3" (Moon) visual approach system.

The advanced design project of the T10-K shipboard fighter was approved in 1984, and prototype construction started. Designated T10K-1, the first prototype (*37 Blue*) was completed in the spring of 1987 and first flew on 17 August piloted by Viktor G. Pugachov. It retained the rigid wings and stabilators of the basic Su-27 because the wing and stabilator folding mechanism still weren't perfected. The second prototype, T10K-2 (*39 Blue*), joined the flight test program almost exactly one year later. This aircraft incorporated all the features.

Both aircraft underwent large-scale testing at Novofyodorovka AB where Sukhoi and NII VVS test pilots perfected the ski jump takeoff and carrier landing techniques. The trials did not go without mishap. The first prototype was lost when it failed to recover from a flat spin.

Carrier compatibility trials were scheduled to begin in the autumn of 1989, even though SNS *Tbilisi* was not 100% complete. Seagoing trials commenced at the end of the month. Before a landing could be risked, Sukhoi and NII VVS pilots trained daily, mastering the unfamiliar no-flare landing technique. The surviving second prototype (T10K-2) and standard Su-27s made low passes over the carrier. Each pilot was to make some 400 landings on the "unsinkable carrier" in Saki before a real-life carrier landing.

SNS *Tbilisi* was a classic aircraft carrier with a straight-through flight deck, an island offset to starboard,

Many test pilots, including Viktor Pugachov (HSU) and Sergey Mel'nikov (Hero of Russia), took part in the Su-27K program. One of the prototypes, T10K-6, is shown here during a test flight. (Yefim Gordon)

The Su-27K (Su-33) differs from the land-based version in having a reinforced landing gear with high-pressure tires. The nose unit has twin wheels. (Yefim Gordon)

and an angled landing deck equipped with a four-wire S-2N arrestor system. The central part of the ship was occupied by the hangar equipped with a turntable and conveyor belts for aircraft handling. Unlike most carriers in the same class, SNS *Tbilisi* had a ski jump on which two takeoff heading lines converged.

On 27 October at about 11 AM, the T10K-2 made an appearance, flying over at about 1,500 m (4,921 ft.). The deck hands watched as it circled, gradually descending, appearing suddenly out of the mist to thunder over the flight deck. Finally Pugachov made a pass along the carrier's port side, waved a hand to greet *Tbilisi's* men, and, after making a barrel roll, made for Saki.

Initially the flights progressed with *Tbilisi* standing at anchor with its

In April 1995 eight Su-27Ks (Su-33s) from Severomorsk were flown to Kubinka to participate in the military parade on the 50th anniversary of the victory in the Great Patriotic War. (Yefim Gordon)

bows to the wind. Later flights were made at 10-13 kts on various headings. On one occasion, when the wind was blowing at 45° on the port beam, the aircraft drifted almost 3 m (10 ft.) to starboard, resulting in a near-accident. Pugachov made a touch-and-go, using the entire deck length, and as

the aircraft cleared the angled deck and the landing gear oleos extended fully, the starboard main wheel struck life line struts on the lesser hull sponson. The struts buckled but the aircraft was undamaged.

The flights resumed on the morning of 1 November, Pugachov

Production Su-27Ks (Su-33s) on the ex-Soviet Naval Aviation Test Centre at Saki, Ukraine. The Saki test center, on the Crimean peninsula in southern Ukraine, was the site for all the carrier trials including those on the dummy deck and ramps. Note the deployed arrestor hook mounted between the nozzles on this Su-27K. Seen on the dummy deck at Saki Naval Aviation Test Center, this Su-27K trials aircraft touches down with its tailhook raised, missing the arrestor cable which lies loose on the runway. All the land-based carrier trials were performed here after delicate negotiations following the breakup of the CIS. (Yefim Gordon)

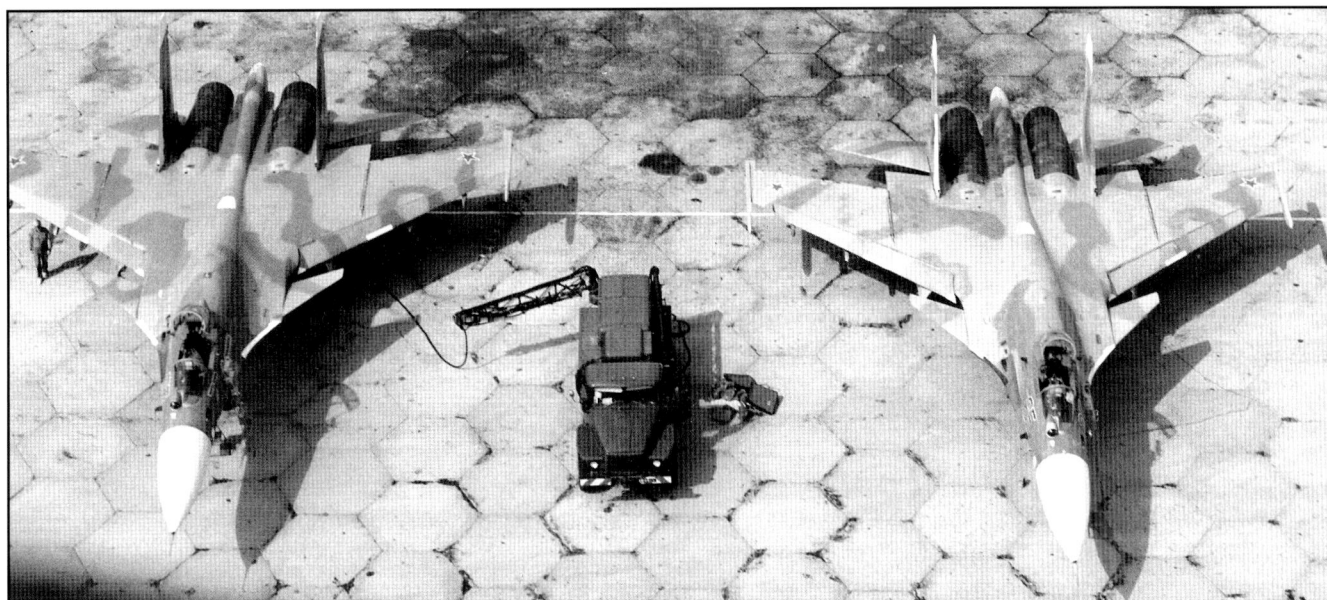

A Su-27K (Su-33) being refueled by a TZ-20 fuel truck. (Yefim Gordon)

flying the T10K-2 and Aubakirov the first prototype MiG-29K (*311 Blue*). The flights were organized so that when one aircraft was on short finals the other was halfway through the landing pattern. At 1:46 PM local time the fighter touched down, catching the second wire, and came to a halt after a landing run of about 90 m (295 ft.). The first conventional carrier landing in the Soviet Union was successfully accomplished.

Thus ended Stage 1 of the trials program: flights were suspended until 10 November while test equipment readings were analyzed. By 10 November, the ship became home to the three aircraft which had flown from it (the T10K-2, the first prototype MiG-29K and the prototype Su-25UTG).

On 21 November Pugachov made the first night landing on the T10K-2, and on the next day the trials program was complete. Between them the participating aircraft had made 227 flights in 24 shifts. In late 1989, even before the MiG-29K and Su-27K had completed their respective flight test programs, the latter aircraft was selected for full-scale production at Komsomol'sk-on-Amur. In the meantime, pre-production aircraft were already rolling off the assembly line there. On 18 August 1991, T10K-4 (*59 Blue*) made the type's public debut at the Aviation Day flypast in Zhukovskiy.

The fifth prototype, *69 Blue*, wore a non-standard overall grey color scheme rather than the usual deep blue of naval Flankers. On 11-16 August 1991, it was on static display at MosAeroShow '92 in Zhukovskiy, carrying a "Moskit" anti-shipping missile. The sixth aircraft (T10K-6, *79 Blue*) was demonstrated to top-ranking military officials at Machoolischchi AB near Minsk on 13 February 1992. The final prototype, T10K-9, wore the three-digit tactical code *109 Blue* – originally on the port side only. This aircraft was displayed at the MAKS-95. The naval version was allocated the code name Flanker- D.

There was a good deal of flying in the summer of 1990 when SNS *Tbilisi* was going through her manufacturer's seagoing trials and state acceptance trials. The navy and the designers tried to get the ship and her aircraft functioning perfectly. Still, the flight test program was not completed in full, despite the fact that three Su-27Ks – the second, third, and fourth prototypes – were now operating from the *Tbilisi* along with other aircraft.

On 4 October 1990 the carrier was renamed, becoming SNS *Admiral Kuznetsov.*

Production Shipboard Fighter Su-27K (Su-33) Flanker-D

In early December 1991, RNS *Admiral Kuznetsov*, commanded by Capt. (1st grade) V. S. Yarygin, sailed from Novorossiysk. The ship was on her way to a new port of registry. With Russia and the Ukraine quarreling over the Black Sea Fleet, it was decided to move the carrier before the Ukraine could lay claim to her.

The Su-27K entered production in Komsomol'sk-on-Amur in 1992. Later the aircraft received the unofficial designation Su-33, and Sukhoi obstinately refers to it as such.

Saki and the "Nitka" training complex were in the newly independent Ukraine, which was at odds with Russia over the Black Sea Fleet issue. This meant that "live" flying from the carrier was the only way of training naval pilots. However, this was obviously impractical because of the increased wear on the carrier and because the military had to negotiate to regain access to the base in Saki. Eventually it was decided that Russia would rent the complex; an agreement was signed and the complex reactivated.

By then aircraft factory No. 99 in Ulan-Ude had completed a small

The aircraft of Russia's only shipboard detachment spend most of their time on dry land. (Yefim Gordon)

Of the 24 shipboard Flankers built to date, only seven production aircraft plus a prototype owned by the Sukhoi OKB participated in the carrier's Mediterranean cruise. (Viktor Drushlyakov)

A production Su-27K (Su-33) makes a training landing on the "Nitka" complex – the "unsinkable carrier" at Saki. (Yefim Gordon)

All production Su-27Ks had a deep blue maritime camouflage. (Yefim Gordon)

With the landing gear just beginning to retract, the Su-27KUB climbs out on a test flight from Zhukovskiy on 21 August 1999. (Yefim Gordon Archive)

The Su-27KUB did not take part in the demonstration flights at the MAKS '99 airshow. On 21 August, however, the spectators had a chance to see it fly. (Yefim Gordon)

batch of production Su-25UTG trainers. In mid 1994 the first 10 pilots of the 279th KIAP (ex 100th KIAP) began flying Su-27Ks and Su-25UTGs from the "unsinkable carrier." In July and August the unit's pilots made 167 arrestor wire engagements and 69 ski jump take-offs. Such intensive training was unheard of even in Soviet times, but this enabled all the unit's pilots to get their carrier rating quickly. By the end of August, all 24 production Su-27Ks (Su-33s) had joined the *Admiral Kuznetsov*.

In the summer of 1995, six Su-27Ks and two Su-25UTGs were "deployed" to Novofyodorovka AB where the first 10 pilots took proficiency training and a fresh group of pilots took the whole course. In October the overhauled carrier took part in a large-scale Northern Fleet exercise. This was the final test before the *Admiral Kuznetsov*'s first long cruise which began on 23 December 1995.

During this cruise a Russian naval delegation paid a visit to the carrier USS *America*; the Americans even gave Maj. Gen. Apakidze a ride in a Grumman A-6 Intruder. Not to be outdone, Russian naval pilots amazed the Americans when two Su-27Ks streaked between RNS *Admiral Kuznetsov* and the missile frigate USS *Monterey* at almost zero level. Maj. Gen. Apakidze also made his mark, giving an impressive aerobatics display.

The cruise revealed numerous shortcomings of both the ship and her aircraft. On one occasion an Su-27K was jumped by Israeli Defense Force/Air Force fighters off the Syrian coast. The IDF/AF jets began hemming the Russian fighter in, as though attempting to force it down on Israeli territory, and the pilot had to make violent maneuvers to break away. The Flanker's avionics had failed to detect the Israeli jets. When the carrier returned to Severomorsk, flights

The Su-27KUB prototype during trials at at Saki AB. Land-based carrier compatibility trials were continued at the Saki test center with the Su-27KUB prototype. The shortened nose and side-by-side seating were better suited to carrier approaches. Trials commenced in 1999 and included approaches, landings, take-offs and go-arounds. (Viktor Drushlyakov)

The Su-27KUB prototype on the carrier's deck. (Viktor Drushlyakov)

wound down to almost nothing. The fighters were grounded by fuel and tire shortages and many malfunctions.

In May 1997 three 279th KIAP pilots went to Zhukovskiy to practice flight refueling techniques. In the summer the unit participated in a Northern Fleet exercise. The group of 12 Flankers destroyed several targets with R-60M (AA-8 *Aphid*) IR-homing "dogfight missiles." This was the first time the Su-27K fired short-range AAMs; not even test pilots had done it before.

Shipboard Trainer Project
Su-27KM-2 (T10KM-2)

A dedicated trainer version of the Su-27K (T10-K) was developed in parallel with the single-seat version. The project was designated T10KM-2 (*korabel'nyy, modifitseerovannyy* – shipboard, modified), but this was rather misleading. Far from being a straightforward adaptation of the land-based Su-27UB (T10-U), the naval trainer had a totally redesigned and much wider forward fuselage

with side-by-side seating for the trainee and instructor. This facilitated crew communication and afforded both crew members an excellent downward field of view – all-important on a carrier.

However, the late '80s defense budget cuts hampered the carrier program. The Navy's interest in the trainer waned, and the project was shelved. Still, the side-by-side seating idea lived on. Sukhoi engineers hoped it would turn the Flanker into a whole family of special-mission aircraft ranging from a shipboard strike aircraft to a tactical recce aircraft to an aerial refueling tanker to an early-warning platform. Ultimately the idea materialized as the Su-27IB/Su-34 tactical bomber.

Shipboard Combat Trainer
Su-27KUB (T10-KU) (Su-33UB)

Operational experience showed that the Su-25UTG was not fully adequate for training Su-27K pilots in takeoff and landing techniques. This

led Sukhoi to dust off the idea of a dedicated naval trainer based on the T10-K. The new project bore the designation T10-KU (*korabel'nyy, oochebnyy* – shipboard trainer). A full-scale mock-up of the forward fuselage was built by KnAAPO and inspected by the Navy.

Funding shortages caused the project to be put on hold, as the Russian MoD was unable to finance development of new military hardware. Fortunately, this situation did not last long. The Flanker-D pilots were growing increasingly vocal about the lack of a trainer version. Thus the T10-KU project was reactivated in 1996, incorporating changes based on Mediterranean cruise experience. More importantly, the ideology of the project changed. The new aircraft was to be a multi-role fighter rather than just a trainer.

The aircraft could best be described as the T10KM-2 project revisited, incorporating major structural and, first of all, aerodynamic changes. These concerned mainly the

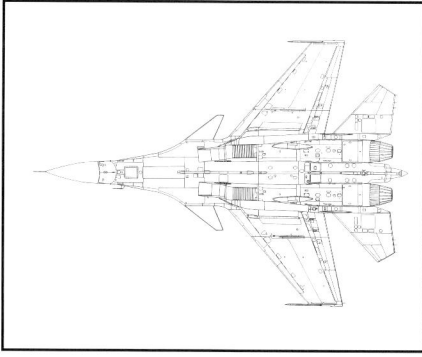

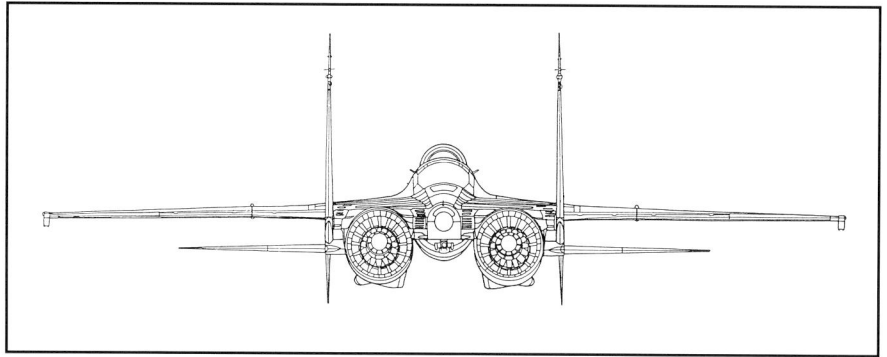

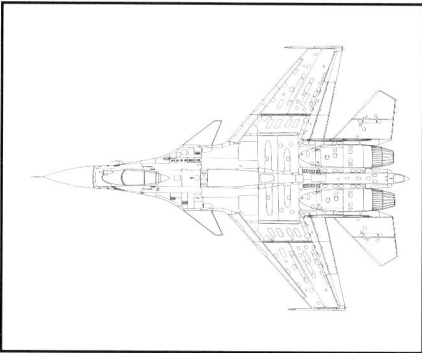

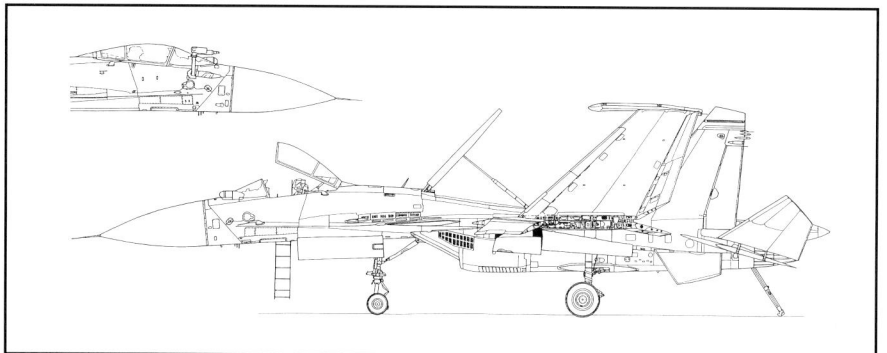

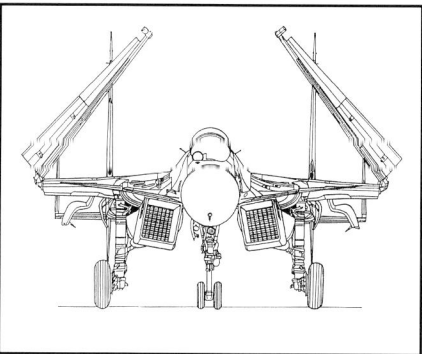

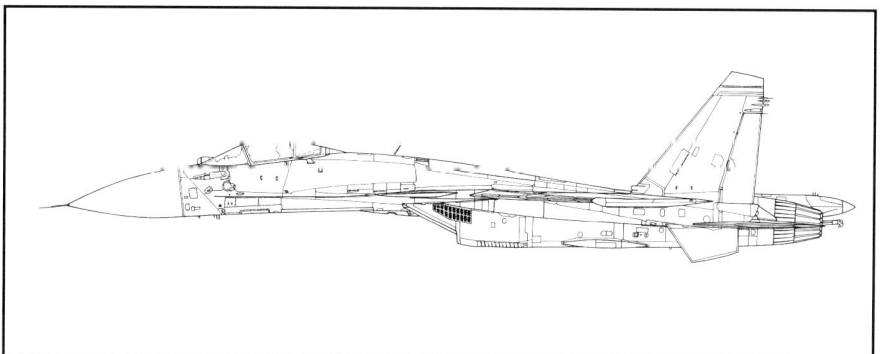

Su-33 line drawings.

wings: span was increased from 14.7 m (48 ft. 2.74 in.) to 16.0 m (52 ft. 5.92 in.) and wing area from 62 m² (666.66 sq. ft.) to 70 m² (752.68 sq. ft.). The T10-KU was the first Russian combat aircraft to feature direct lift control. The high-lift devices adapted automatically to the prevailing flight conditions. This provided optimum lift in cruise mode, improving agility and increasing range. A special elastic seal closed the gap between the LE flaps and the wings, ensuring smooth airflow when the flaps were down.

The wing folding joints were moved outboard approximately 1.5 m

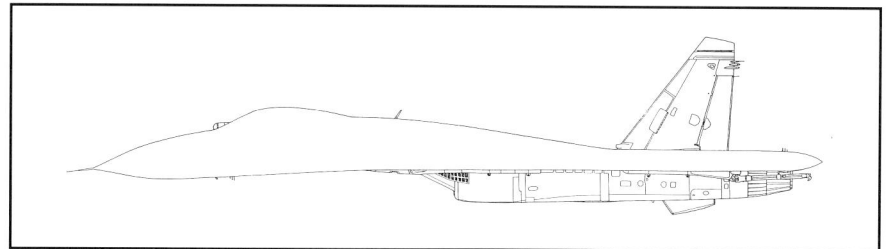

(4 ft. 11 in.) on each side so that the inner wingspan matched the horizontal tail span; thus the T10-KU required slightly more space for deck/hangar storage as compared to the Su-27K. The wing folding angles were reduced, the outer wings being almost vertical when folded. The canards were enlarged and reshaped (their tips were no longer parallel to the fuselage axis; this measure was meant to aid

stealth). Horizontal tail area and rudder area were also increased. Unlike the production Su-27K, the aircraft did not have folding stabilators.

The forward fuselage was heavily modified. The T10-KU had a Su-34-style cockpit with side-by-side seating accessed from below via the nose wheel well. Apart from the reasons mentioned previously (crew communication and visibility), this arrange-

Two views of the repainted Su-27KUB prototype. (Yefim Gordon)

Repainted Su-27KUB prototype makes a demonstration flight at the MAKS-2003 airshow. (Yefim Gordon)

ment was chosen because in an aircraft with stepped-tandem seating the back-seater would find it hard to use the VASI. This is important, since an aircraft carrier's VASI imposes strict limits on the pilot's eye level during final approach. In the T10-KU, both crewmembers enjoyed almost identical conditions.

The "hump" aft of the cockpit was not as pronounced as on the Su-34. Also, an IRST "ball" (absent on the bomber version) was installed ahead of the windscreen; unlike the Su-27K, it was located on the centerline, not offset to starboard. The production T10-KU makes use of LLLTV and thermal imaging equipment, as well as a self-contained precision navigation system.

Wearing no tactical code, the prototype was rolled out in the spring of

1999. On 29 April 1999 the Su-27KUB successfully made its first flight in Zhukovskiy with pilot Viktor G. Pugachov and WSO Sergey Mel'nikov at the controls. Manufacturer's flight tests continued until mid-summer 2000. In late summer 1999 the Su-27KUB paid a visit to Novofyodorovka AB, Saki, to make its first ski-jump takeoffs and carrier landings on the Nitka RDTC. In the autumn of 1999 the aircraft commenced carrier compatibility trials aboard the *Admiral Kuznetsov*.

The Su-27KUB is doubtlessly a major step in the development of Russian shipboard aircraft. Despite the bigger fuselage cross-section area, it has much more refined aerodynamics than the production Su-27K. As compared to the latter aircraft, the lift/drag ratio is improved more than

10%, mainly thanks to the smart adaptive wings with the flexible LE that, together with the flaperons, continuously optimizes the airfoil for maximum efficiency.

Data presentation systems and controls received special attention when the Su-27KUB's cockpit was designed. The little cube makes use of the dark cockpit principle. This means the aircraft's systems do not distract the crew with warning lights if everything is normal. For the same reason the number of buttons, switches, etc., have been kept to a minimum, allowing the crew to concentrate on the mission. For the time being, both a traditional control stick and a sidestick are under consideration; a special trials program is being held in order to make the selection.

The Su-27KUB is the first Russian fighter to have a liquid oxygen converter that can also generate gaseous nitrogen. This reduces the need for ground (shipboard) support equipment and maintenance personnel.

T10KU-1 was test-flown by Indian pilots in September 1999 but was judged too large for the planned carriers. Any production is likely to be by KnAAPO after investigation of trainer, reconnaissance and AEW versions, the last-mentioned with a phased-array mounted on the spine, between the composite antenna tailfins. Increased thrust, thrust-vectoring AL-31FP, AL-31FM, or AL-4 IF engines were mooted for production version.

THE SU-27 IN COLOR

This hangar, along with the protection boxes for the engine intakes shielded the aircraft T10-1 from U.S. surveillance satellites at the Sukhoi test center although the open sides allowed extremes of weather free access. (Sukhoi OKB archive)

T10-1, 10 Blue in the spring of 1977 showing the early forward hinged main gear doors and forward positioned nose-gear. (Sukhoi OKB archive)

A spectacular image of T10-17 over a typical Russian snows-cape carrying wingtip AAMs during state acceptance trials. (Sukhoi OKB archive)

All versions of the Flanker feature access to the radar set by raising the nosecone with a special jack. (Sukhoi OKB archive)

Parked up for a picture, the first prototype Su-30 (T10PU-5) forces the company photographer down in the ice for this interesting angle. (Sukhoi OKB archive)

Seen from below and bristling with heavy munitions, the first prototype Su-30MKI carries 32 250-kg FAB-250 bombs on MBD3-u6-68 multiple ejector racks and two R-73 AAMs on the wingtip pylons (Sukhoi OKB)

Carrying weapons for the interceptor role, 501 Blue, the first real prototype Su-30MKK is seen during a test flight. The vectoring nozzles are in tapered mode. (Viktor Drushlyakov)

The second and third Su-30MKKs, 502 Blue and 503 Black in formation during a test flight (Sukhoi OKB)

WARBIRDTECH
SERIES

T10M-9 (709 Black *outline*), the ninth prototype Su-27M, was painted in a more tropical "splinter camouflage" for a demonstration tour of the Middle East and SE Asia featuring all the usual Cobra maneuvers. (Yefim Gordon)

Yevgeni Frolov effectively demonstrates the enhanced maneuverability of the thrust-vectoring Russian fighter. (Sukhoi OKB)

The vectoring nozzle of the AL-31FU bleeds down after engine shutdown. (Yefim Gordon)

Featuring a new black, white and gray disruptive color scheme, Su-27SKM 305 Black prototype is seen on the ramp before a test flight. (Sukhoi OKB)

The second prototype, T10K-2 (39 Blue). (Yefim Gordon archive)

A real navalized Flanker, fifth prototype, T10K-5 (69 Blue), at MosAeroShow '92 in Zhukovskiy. Note the landing lights in the nosegear well and the deployed refueling probe. (Yefim Gordon)

The full-size mockup of the T10-K; T10-20KTM; which was used for hangar compatibility tests. Note the very basic wing hinge, folded stabilator and the absence of canards. It is interesting that the mezzanine engineering offices are so close to the real thing. (Sukhoi OKB archive)

All Su-27Ks are equipped with a retractable refueling probe. (Yefim Gordon)

Wings and stabilator folded during the taxi run show how the Su-27K can be ready for instant stowage during hectic carrier operations. (Yefim Gordon)

This Su-33, 86 Red, also participated in the Mediterranean cruise. (Yefim Gordon)

The platypus nose and broad side-by-side cockpit arrangement of this, the first production-standard Su-34 (T10V-2, 43 Blue) can be seen from this elevated viewpoint. (Yefim Gordon)

A spectacular view of two of eight Su-27Ks (Su-33s) flown to Kubinka for the 50th anniversary of the victory in the Great Patriotic War in April 1995. The flying control positions for an afterburner take-off can be seen clearly. (Yefim Gordon)

The Su-27KUB leaves the T-2 ski jump of the unsinkable carrier at Saki AB. (Viktor Drushlyakov)

Afterburners blazing, the Su-27KUB clears the ski jump of the Admiral Kuznetsov carrier. (Viktor Drushlyakov)

SUKHOI
SU-27 FLANKER

69

Early morning scene on the Admiral Kuznetsov. (Viktor Drushlyakov)

Seen totally clean with no stores, this view of T10V-5 shows its aerodynamic form to great effect. Note the twin nose wheel and double bogie main gear. (Yefim Gordon)

The T10V-5's rather yucky "greenbottle fly" camouflage is effective for over-water sorties. (Yefim Gordon)

Su-34 production in Novosibirsk. (Vestnik Vozdooshnovo Flota)

The Su-34 (Air Force designation Su-27IB) had its debut in 2000, taking part in a Russian Air Force exercise. (Sukhoi OKB)

The Roosskiye Vityazi (Russian Knights) aerobatic team also flies two Su-27UB trainers. (Yefim Gordon)

A Su-27UB taxies at Lipetsk training center. (Yefim Gordon)

WARBIRDTECH
S E R I E S

Kvochur's Su-27P executing a high-G turn. (Yefim Gordon)

The retractable refueling probe of the Su-30 shown in the stowed position. The cockpit proximity makes the hook-up relatively straightforward in all weathers. (Sukhoi OKB archive)

The Russian Knights in "arrow" formation show their national colors to the crowd.

This Ukrainian AF Su-27 performed at many airshows, including the Royal International Air Tattoo at RAF Fairford, England, the world's largest military airshow. (Yefim Gordon archive)

R-60M "dogfight missiles" are usually carried on the outer wing pylons. These short-range AA-8 Aphid AAMs were first fired on the Su-27K in a Northern Fleet exercise in 1997. (Yefim Gordon)

The cockpit interior of a single-seat Su-27. The red lever to the right jettisons the canopy. The magnetic compass is fixed to the canopy frame beside the HUD. (Sukhoi OKB archive)

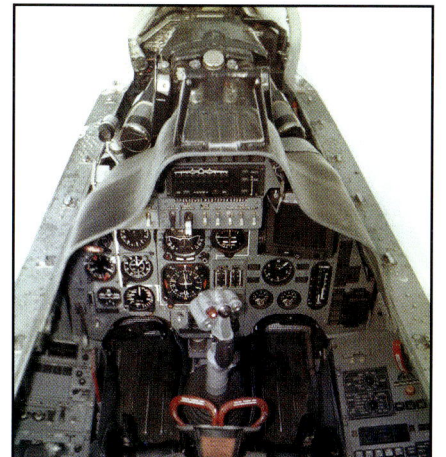

The instructor's cockpit of a Su-27UB. The rear cockpit enjoys a reasonable field of view over the forward one due to its raised position. (Sukhoi OKB archive)

Seen at Aero India 2005 at Yehelanka Air Base near Bangalore, this locally assembled Flanker with its computer-controlled vectoring nozzles even uses them for taxiing, steering, and acceleration. This variant is arguably the most advanced fighter in the world at this time. (Peter Davison)

This Ukrainian Air Force Flanker approaches Brno airport in the Czech Republic after stealing the show at the Czech Air Fest in 2004. Ukrainian Flankers regularly appear at large East European air displays, always giving impressive performances. (Peter Davison)

WARBIRD**TECH**
S E R I E S

LARGE COCKPIT GENERATION

The T10V-1 (Su-27IB) prototype, 42 Blue, near the Sukhoi hangar in Zhukovskiy. (Yefim Gordon)

The Su-27IB's characteristic "platypus nose" with sharp chines incorporates stealth technology. (Yefim Gordon)

Tactical Fighter-Bomber Prototype Su-27IB (T10V-1)

In the mid 80s the Sukhoi OKB was facing a major challenge. A multirole tactical aircraft was required. It was to be fast, have good maneuverability, long range, and a high payload. These seemingly contradictory requirements could only be met by making use of the latest breakthroughs in aerodynamics, manufacturing technology, avionics, and weapons.

The engineers selected the Su-27 fighter, which had just entered production, as the basis for the fourth-generation strike aircraft. Developed as a replacement for the Su-24M Fencer-D tactical bomber, the aircraft bore the designation T10-V.

Mikhail P. Simonov supervised the program, while Rolan G. Martirosov was the chief project engineer.

Specialist design bureaus were also involved. The mission avionics suite was subcontracted to NPO "Leninets" led by General Designer G. N. Gromov. Three design bureaus – "Vympel" under G. A. Sokolovskiy, "Zvezda" (Star) under G. I.

Khokhlov, and "Raduga" (Rainbow) under I. S. Seleznyov – were responsible for the armament.

The T10-V was a rework of the stillborn T10KM-2 naval trainer project with the all-new forward fuselage and side-by-side seating. This arrangement made the aircraft more suitable for the bomber, tanker, recce, ECM, and other roles. Unlike the basic Su-27 which had a circular-section forward fuselage, the T10-V had a flattened nose with sharp chines reminiscent of the Lockheed SR-71 Blackbird, which continued aft until they blended into the LERXes. This promptly gave rise to the nickname *Ootkonos* (platypus).

The cockpit was accessed from behind via the nose wheel well by means of a retractable ladder. For survivability the forward fuselage was a built as a capsule of titanium armor up to 17 mm (0.67 in.) thick. The fuselage fuel tank and the engine nacelles were also protected. The armor weighed 1,480 kg (3,262 lbs.), so the nose gear had twin wheels and retracted aft. For cockpit access, the wheel well had four doors instead of the usual one.

To improve maneuverability and field performance, the T10-V was equipped with canards, which meant the LERXes had to be extended forward. The adjustable supersonic air intakes of the fighter version gave way to simple fixed-area intakes, and the ventral fins were deleted. The AL-31F engines were replaced by AL-31FMs uprated to 12,800 kgp (28,218 lb st) in full afterburner and equipped with full authority digital engine control (FADEC). The number of external stores hard points was increased to 12.

The first prototype, T10V-1 (*42 Blue*), was converted from a standard Su-27UB. The T10V-1 made its first flight in Zhukovskiy on 13 April 1990 at the hands of distinguished test pilot

A 3/4 front view of the T10V-1 (Su-27IB). This tactical fighter bomber prototype owes its cockpit and nose profile to the naval trainer but has the additional canard foreplanes and extended chines. (Yefim Gordon)

A side view of the T10V-1 (Su-27IB). The cockpit was enclosed in an armored titanium capsule. The fuel tank and engine nacelles were also reinforced. This extra weight resulted in undercarriage modifications including a twin nose wheel. (Yefim Gordon)

The Su-27IB's show debut was at Machoolischchi on 13 February 1992. (ITAR-TASS)

Anatoliy Ivanov, one of the company's best pilots. The manufacturer's flight test program took all of 1990 and continued into 1991. Later the first prototype was officially designated Su-27IB, the suffix letters denoting *istrebeetel'-bombardirovschchik* (fighter-bomber).

The OKB built numerous test rigs to verify the Su-27IB's new systems. One for testing the brake parachute system featured a real Flanker airframe with a retractable brake chute container. Powerful fans placed in front of it simulated the slipstream. Special care was given to the crew escape system that was tested on a forward fuselage attached to a rocket-powered sled.

The Su-27IB was officially unveiled at Machoolischchi AB near Minsk on 13 February 1992. The latest

WARBIRD**TECH**
SERIES

To accommodate the pilot and WSO side by side, the Su-27IB's forward fuselage had to be widened. (Sukhoi OKB)

The Su-27IB made demo flights at MosAeroShow '92, piloted by Yevgeni Revunov and Yevgeni Donchenko. (Yefim Gordon)

military aircraft were displayed to the leaders of the CIS to impress the President and release additional funds for the program so that further prototypes could be built. The Su-27IB was demonstrated to the general public at MosAeroShow '92 and MAKS '93. The Su-27IB gave a brief aerobatics display, demonstrating excellent handling.

Photos published after the show gave Western experts a fairly good idea of the aircraft's capabilities.

Multi-Role Tactical Strike Aircraft (T10-V Su-34/Su-32FN)

The second prototype, T10V-2 (*43 Blue*), made its first flight in Novosibirsk on 18 December 1993. This was the first Su-27IB in production configuration, and it had enough changes to warrant a new service designation, Su-34.

The heavier Su-34 had the same integral layout as the rest of the Flanker family, the most obvious difference being the landing gear. The single main wheels were replaced with twin bogies located in tandem as on the SAAB Viggen. This was particularly important when landing with a partially used weapons load and on unprepared tactical airstrips, albeit at a reduced MTOW. The bogies rotated 180° forward during retraction to lie lengthwise in the wing roots.

The tail "stinger" was much longer and fatter than the Su-27IB's and ended in a large dielectric fairing, indicating provision for a rearward

warning radar. Apart from the warning function, the radar could guide AAMs capable of destroying not only aircraft but guided missiles as well – a feature not currently found on any Western strike aircraft. Installation of the radar meant that the brake parachute container had to be moved forward because it popped up when the chute deployed.

The Su-34 is unique among tactical fighter-bombers in regards to crew comfort. "Cockpit" is hardly the word to describe its crew quarters. It is really a flight deck. A galley and a toilet are located aft of the crew seats. A powerful air conditioning system automatically maintains air pressure at 2,400 m (7,874 ft.) for flight levels up to 10,000 m (32,808 ft.), enabling work without using oxygen masks. Thus, mission time can be extended to 10 hours, boosting the Su-34's combat potential.

Like the basic Flanker, the Su-34 has digital FBW control, and it also features an active flight safety and pitch stabilization system. The pitch stabilization system linked to the canards gives the aircraft a smooth ride. There is also a panic button function. The aircraft is brought to straight and level flight from any attitude with one button. The system incorporates artificial intelligence, automatically monitoring the pilots' physical condition, systems status, and fuel quantity. It also enables automatic return to base and runway approach.

The airframe makes use of stealth technology. The radome has sharp chines blending into the LERXes. Together with the integral layout, this decreases the aircraft's radar cross-section (RCS) while ensuring good aerodynamics. This is further helped by radar-absorbent coatings and the deletion of the ventral fins. The Su-34's RCS is much lower than that of the Su-24, F-111, and F-15E; in low-level flight it is approximately equal to that of a modern cruise missile.

The aircraft is equipped with a completely new computerized navigation suite that can be set to fly automatically to a given location with an accuracy of 1 m (3 ft.). It includes an inertial navigation system (INS), radio navigation aids, and GPS. The flight deck features multi-mode color cathode-ray tube (CRT) displays, as well as HUDs. In addition, the pilot and navigator have helmet-mounted sights for use with point-and-shoot weapons. The radar is capable of detecting aerial targets, including small ones, at a range of 250 km (138 nm).

In maritime patrol/ASW configuration the Su-34 relies mainly on radar and sonobuoys, as well as FLIR, laser ranging equipment, and low light-level TV systems. For ASW duties, the aircraft carries up to 72 active and passive sonobuoys operating within a broad spectrum of frequencies, as well as explosive sound sources (small bombs which generate sound waves).

The Su-34 is heavier than the pure fighter versions of the Flanker (the MTOW is 45,000 kg/99,206 lbs. and normal TOW is 42,000 kg/92,592 lbs.), yet performance has deteriorated only slightly in

The first production-standard Su-34 strike aircraft (T10V-2, 43 Blue). This photo was taken in the winter of 1993-94, and the snowy conditions highlight the strengthened undercarriage with twin wheel bogies and tandem main gear as in the Saab Viggen, similarly designed for northern latitudes. (Yefim Gordon)

3/4 port view of the T10V-5 taken at the Zhukovsky flight test center near Moscow. The rugged undercarriage and crew access through the nose wheel bay is clearly visible. (Yefim Gordon)

In addition to the tactical code (45 White outline), the T10V-5 carries the Le Bourget '95 exhibit code 349. (Yefim Gordon)

comparison with the Su-27 and Su-30. As in the fighter versions, never-exceed speed is 1,400 km/h (777 kts) at sea level and Mach 1.8 at high altitude.

The first flight of Su-34, *43 Blue*, on 18 December 1993, lasted 52 minutes.

In the first days of June 1995, *45 White* arrived at LII for a brush-up

The aft-retracting nose gear unit has twin wheels and a beefed-up oleo. (Yefim Gordon)

The Su-27IB taking on fuel from the Il-78M prototype, SSSR-76701. (Sergey Skrynnikov)

The Su-34 (T10V-2) had revised main gear units with tandem-wheel bogies replacing the single mainwheels of the Su-27IB (T10V-1). (Yefim Gordon)

prior to its appearance at Le Bourget. Painted a rather shocking iridescent green, the aircraft was demonstrated to Mikhail Simonov and officials a few days before the departure. However, the demo – the T10V-5's 18th flight – nearly ended in disaster as the main gear units would not extend at the end of the flight. Luckily, the pilots (Igor' Votintsev and Igor' Solovyov) realized what was happening and made a steep left turn over the runway, and the G force wrenched the landing gear loose. The aircraft landed with parts of the main gear units dangling from the wheel wells.

Spares were rushed from Novosibirsk to replace the damaged components, and after hasty repairs the T10V-5 flew to Le Bourget wearing the exhibit code 349. Interestingly, the tablet in front of the aircraft identified it as Su-32FN – probably an export designation for the type. Sukhoi chose to keep the aircraft in the static park throughout the show – quite wisely, as it suffered more malfunctions on the return trip.

On 22-27 August of the same year, the T10V-5 was displayed at the MAKS '95 airshow – once again only in the static park. Some of the visitors dubbed it, rather unkindly, *Greenbottle Fly*, referring to the bright green color scheme. This camouflage appears to have been selected for the naval version, being more effective over water. The third flying Su-34, T10V-4, entered flight test in early 1997, also wearing this color scheme and low-viz tactical code (*44 White* outline). In June 1997 it was displayed at Le Bourget with the exhibit code 343.

If, despite Russia's current economic plight, funding of the Su-34 program continues, the Russian Air Force gets a very capable combat aircraft to defend the country's land and maritime borders more efficiently and at lower costs. The Su-34 (Su-32FN) also has considerable export potential.

The Su-34 in Detail

The Su-34 has a totally new forward fuselage, reinforced wings and vertical tails. It features canards like the Su-27K and Su-35 but lacks ventral fins. The landing gear is completely different. The Su-34 has simple fixed-area air intakes that decrease performance slightly but save weight and make room for the bulkier main gear. It has an integral layout. The low-aspect-ratio wings with pronounced LERXes blend with the fuselage to create a single lifting body. The main gear fairings continue aft into the tail unit attachment beams.

Fuselage

The fuselage is integral with the wing center section. The forward fuselage includes an elliptical-section radome with sharp chines. It incorporates the flight deck, nose wheel well, and an equipment bay for the refueling probe. The radome terminates in a long pitot boom mounting navigational aerials and (on prototypes only) additional pitch and yaw vanes. A Q-bay aft of the flight deck accommodates most of the aircraft's avionics on racks and the ammo box of the built-in gun.

The center fuselage houses the main integral fuel tanks. Two hard points are located in tandem in the tunnel between the nacelles. The fixed-area air intakes of slightly rounded rectangular section are attached to the underside of the LERXes. The intake upper lip/fixed intake ramp acts as a boundary layer splitter plate. The intakes feature auxiliary blow-in/spill doors.

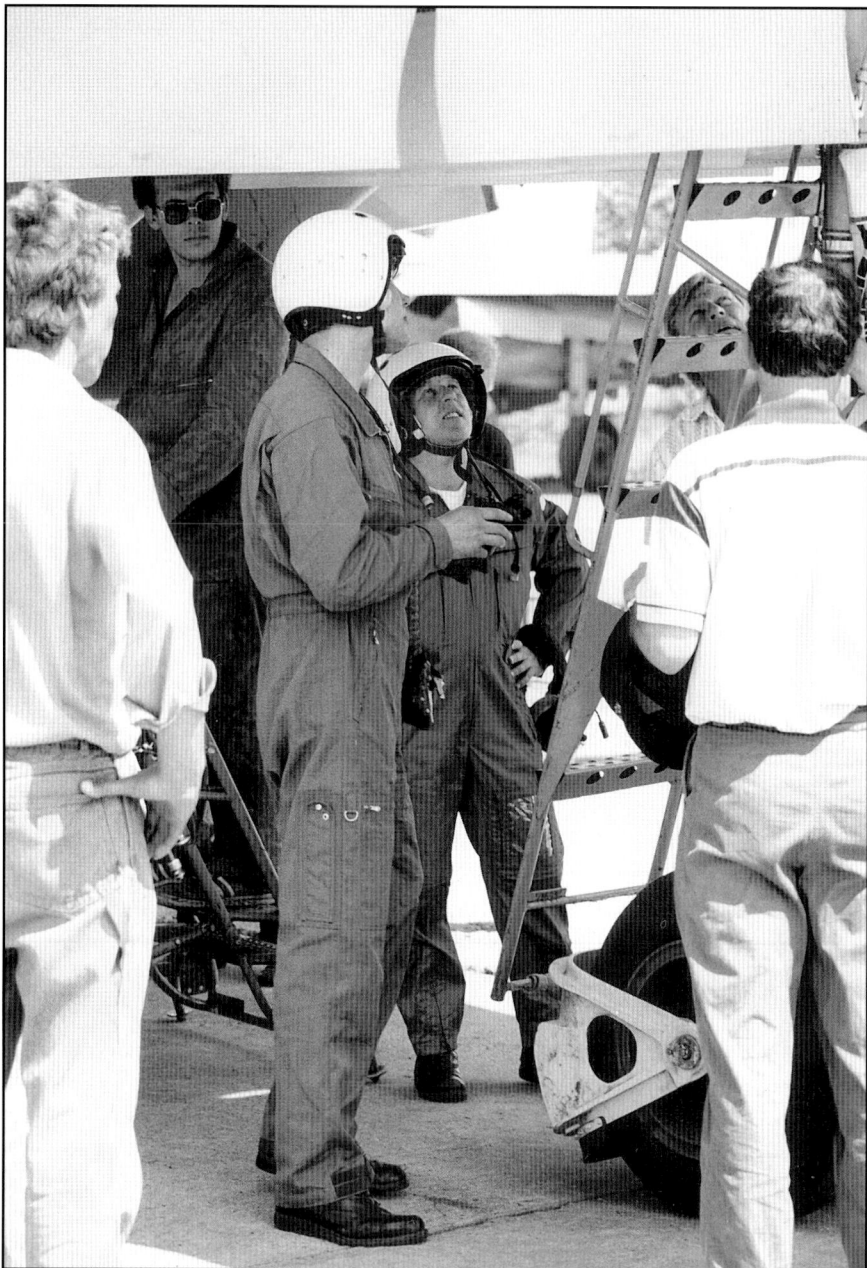

Technicians inspecting the T10V-5 after a near-accident. (Yefim Gordon)

The fifth Flanker bomber that commenced flight tests in Novosibirsk in December 1996 was the first T10-V to be equipped with a fire-control radar. (Vestnik Vozdooshnovo Flota)

The Su-34 (T10V-4) gets unstuck; a tight turn to the left usually comes next. (Yefim Gordon Archive)

The aft fuselage comprises two engine bays, tail unit attachment beams, and the tail stinger, which is the central structural member. The nacelles have removable dorsal access panels for maintenance. The two rearmost nacelle mainframes are built in two portions each and are opened for engine removal. The tail stinger terminating in a dielectric fairing contains the aft fuel tank, the retractable brake parachute container, and an avionics bay for a rear warning radar or a magnetic anomaly detector. The tail unit attachment beams incorporate fittings for the fins and stabilators, as well as equipment bays housing stabilator actuators, etc.

Wings

Wings are cantilever mid-wing monoplane of blended wing/body design, built in three sections (integral center section and two outer wings). Leading edge sweep 42°, aspect ratio 3.5, taper 3.4.

The wings are equipped with two-section LE flaps with an area of 4.6 m² (49.46 sq. ft.) and flaperons with an area of 4.9 m² (52.68 sq. ft.) that are deflected in takeoff/landing mode or during maneuvering. LE flap deflection is 30°, flaperon deflection is +35°/-20°.

The outer wings are three-spar structures with integral fuel tanks. Each outer wing has four weapons hard points, including the wingtip missile rail that can be removed and replaced with an ECM pod. The center section accommodates the main gear units. The port LERX houses avionics while the starboard houses the 30-mm single-barrel gun and incorporates cooling louvres. A heat-resistant steel panel is fitted ahead of the gun muzzle to protect the skin from hot gun-blast gases.

The one-piece canard foreplanes have an LE sweep of 53°30', a span of 6.4 m (21 ft.), and an area of approximately 3 m² (32.25 sq. ft.).

Tail Unit

The Su-27 has differentially movable stabilizers for pitch and roll control (stabilators). The trapezoidal stabilators have an LE sweep of 45°; stabilator span is 9.8 m (32 ft. 1.82 in.) and area is 12.2 m² (131.18 sq. ft.). For pitch control the stabilators are deflected +20° through -15°; for roll control they are deflected with a 10° difference.

The twin vertical tails are also mounted on the tail unit attachment beams. Total vertical tail area is 15.4 m² (165.59 sq. ft.), leading-edge sweep is 40°. The rudders, of area 1.75 m² (18.8 sq. ft.) each, can be deflected 25°. The fin tips and the starboard fin LE are formed by dielectric fairings over the aerials.

Landing Gear

The landing gear is a hydraulically retractable tricycle type. The forward-retracting telescopic main units have twin-wheel bogies with tandem KT-206 brake wheels. Because of a skewed retraction hinge, each main wheel leg rotates through 90° during retraction so that the wheels lie horizontally. At the same time, the bogie rotates 90° around the leg to stow fore and aft in the wing center section with the rear wheel foremost. Landing gear wheelbase and track are 6.6

The Su-34's canards and computerized state-of-the-art active flight safety system enhance maneuverability and give the aircraft a smooth ride in turbulent conditions. (Sergey Skrynnikov)

m (21 ft. 7.84 in.) and 4.4 m (14 ft. 5.2 in.), respectively.

Engine

The engine is basically similar to that of the Su-27: two Lyul'ka AL-21F-3 afterburning turbojets rated at 7,800 kgp (17,195 lb st) dry and 11,200 kgp (24,691 lb st) reheat located in spaced nacelles on the fuselage underside.

Fuel System

The fuel system comprises four integral fuel tanks – three in the fuselage and one in the wings. Internal fuel volume is increased as compared to the Su-27/Su-30. Two of the wing pylons are wet, permitting the carriage of drop tanks. Additionally, the Su-34 is equipped with a retractable refueling probe located offset to port and illuminated by retractable lights for night refueling.

Hydraulics

Hydraulics consist of two independent closed-type hydraulic systems, each with its own engine-driven pump. The hydraulic system caters for the control system, landing gear operation and wheel braking, wing LE and TE flap operation, and air intake FOD grille operation.

Pneumatic and Environmental Control Systems

These systems are similar to those of the Su-27. An inclined K-36DM ejection seat mitigates the effect of high G loads. The high-capacity oxygen system and food and water and waste containers are provided for long sorties.

Electrics

Electrics are similar to those of the Su-27. An auxiliary power unit (APU) keeps the systems operational

in the event of engine failure. The AL-31F features a full-authority analogue engine control system and a backup hydro-mechanical control system.

Crew Rescue System and Crew Gear

The aircraft is equipped with two standardized K-36DM Srs 2 zero-zero ejection seats to ensure safe ejection within the flight envelope. Two upper sections of the canopy are jettisoned before ejection.

Armament

Armament consists of a single GSh-301 30-mm quick-firing single-barrel gun with 150 rounds and a wide variety of guided or unguided missiles and bombs on 12 hard points. Air-to-air weapons options include up to six medium- and long-range R-27 (AA-10 *Alamo*) AAMs – radar-homing (R-27R1, R-27ER) or IR-homing (R-27T, R-27ET) – up to eight

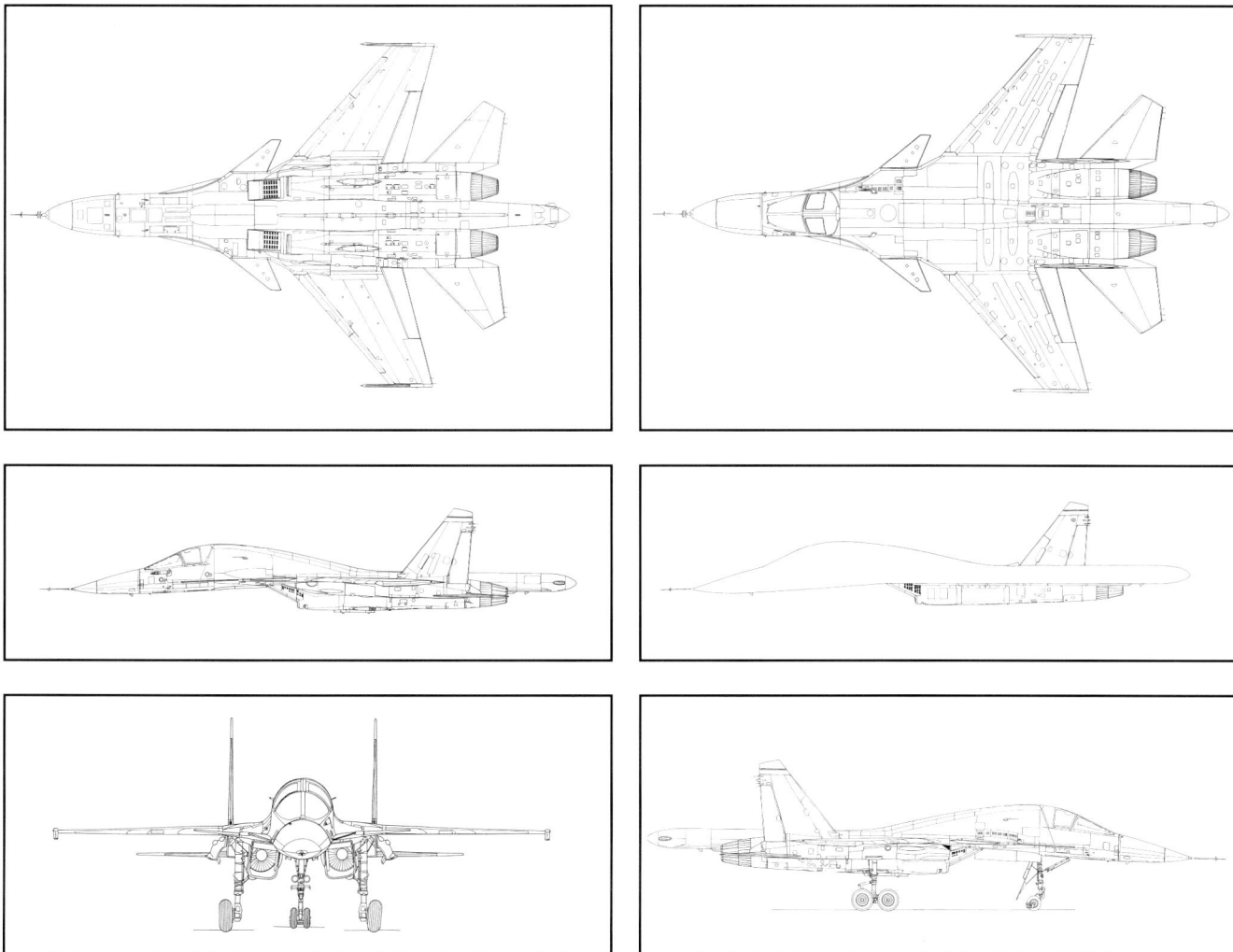

Su-34 line drawings.

R-77 (RVV-AE/AA-12 *Adder*) medium-range AAMs with a combined guidance system, and up to six R-73 (AA-11 *Archer*) IR-homing short-range AAMs.

Guided air-to-ground weapons include Kh-25M (AS-10 *Karen*) and Kh-29 (AS-14 *Kedge*) missiles, S-25L missiles, Kh-31A medium-range anti-shipping missiles and Kh-31P anti-radiation missiles, Kh-59M TV-guided missiles, and KAB-500 and KAB-1500 smart bombs (500 kg/1,102 lbs. and 1,500 kg/3,306 lbs. respectively) in laser-guided and TV-guided versions. The Su-34 can carry up to three Kh-59M missiles or KAB-1500 bombs, or up to six missiles or bombs of the other models.

The naval version is armed with two 3M80 "Moskit" (ASM-MSS) anti-shipping missiles or three "Alpha" (AFM-L) ASMs. The "Moskit" weighs 4,000 kg (8,818 lbs.), has a 250-km (138-nm) range, and a Mach 3 cruising speed. The 1,500-kg (3,306-lb) "Alpha" has a range of 300 km (166 nm) and a cruising speed of Mach 2.2-3.0.

The Su-34 can also carry ordinary "dumb bombs" weighing from 100 to 500 kg (220-1,102 lbs.), KMGU submunitions pods, and unguided rockets. The maximum ordnance load is 8,000 kg (17.636 lbs.).

Avionics and Equipment

Production Su-34s differ in mission equipment fit, depending on whether the air force or the navy operates the aircraft. Target information is presented on the two head-up displays and on multi-function liquid-crystal displays.

The navigation and flight instrumentation suite includes an air data system, an autopilot and autolanding system, an INS, a Doppler speed and drift sensor, a satellite navigation system (GPS), short-range (SHORAN) and long-range (LORAN) radio navaids, a marker beacon receiver, an IFF transponder, and flight data/cockpit voice recorders used to evaluate mission success or reconstruct an accident. The defensive equipment suite includes ELINT and ECM pods, an infrared missile warning system detecting incoming missiles by their heat signature, and chaff/flare dispensers.

OPERATIONAL FLANKERS

The Su-27 officially joined the VVS and IA PVO inventory in 1984. The first official acknowledgement of the Su-27's existence came in the summer of 1985. A documentary about Pavel O. Sukhoi, shown on Soviet TV to mark the designer's 90th anniversary, included a brief reference and a 10-second sequence showing the T10-1 on take-off. However, it was another two years before the first photos of a real production Su-27 appeared.

The 941st IAP[14], a unit of the 10th PVO Air Army stationed up north on the Kola Peninsula near the Norwe-gian border, was one of the first to convert to the Su-27P. In the autumn of 1987 one of its aircraft, *36 Red*, became famous when Western aerospace magazines published dramatic close-up shots of it carry-ing a full complement of R-27T and R-27ER missiles.

LII test pilot Anatoliy Kvochur established the "Istrebeeteli" (Fighters) aerobatic team flying Flankers – two single-seat Su-27Ps and two probe-equipped Su-30 two-seaters. They wear the Russian flag colors of white, blue, and red and are painted with West-ern enamels. (Yefim Gordon)

Two aircraft of the "Istrebeeteli" team and the Su-27IB with the Il-78M prototype SSSR-76701 in a simulated three-ship refueling. (Yefim Gordon archive)

The undersides of the Su-27s flown by the Rooskiye Vityazi (Russian Knights) aerobatic team are painted in Russian national colors. (Yefim Gordon)

RC-135 ELINT platforms and other Western military aircraft logged more than 72 hours in the 10th Air Army's area of responsibility. On four occasions, Su-27Ps scrambled to intercept possible intruders.

Maj. Yevgeniy Oleynik, deputy Sqn. Ldr. of 1 Sqn/941st IAP, recalls flying top cover for marine forces holding live firing training in 1996. "I was all alone out over international waters and a good long way from the shore when a pair of F-16s popped up and, in a manner of speaking, asked me to step outside. They came within 50 m (164 ft.). I could see the pilots' faces covered by oxygen masks. We were all armed with missiles. We followed parallel courses for a while, then started showing each other what our aircraft can do – wingovers, yo-yos, and so on. It was a sort of mock combat. However, the tussle was brief, as at 10,000 m (32,808 ft.) the Su-27 has an advantage over the F-16. Pretty soon the 'guests' departed and I was all alone again. It felt good to know that they gave up and didn't scare me off. Still, it's quite possible they were merely getting low on fuel."

Insufficient training and the resulting lack of proficiency sometimes ended in tragedy. On 11 August 1994, a Russian Air Force Su-27 crashed near Khabarovsk, killing the 28-year-old pilot. On 1 October 1997, a 941st IAP Su-27UB crashed near its home base during a training sortie.

The Su-27 has never fired in anger but it has seen action. Apart from keeping Western spy planes in check on the northern frontiers, VVS Su-27s were used in the closing stages of the Afghan war. The Flankers flew top cover for strike aircraft near the Pakistani border but did not actually engage in combat with PAF fighters. Russian forces used later Su-27s

By late 1990, when the Conventional Forces in Europe (CFE) treaty was signed, 138 VVS Flankers and 229 more Su-27Ps operated by the PVO were based in the European part of the USSR. Of these, the Russian Air Force and Air Defense Force retained

little more than 100 after the breakup of the Soviet Union.

In just three months of 1997, the Russian PVO's 10th Air Army radar units detected and tracked the movements of 20 "ferret" aircraft and 141 foreign combat aircraft. P-3s, Boeing

during the civil war in Georgia. Abkhazi separatists shot down one aircraft. Starting 21 December 1994, two to six Flankers and MiG-31 Foxhound interceptors patrolled the airspace over the breakaway republic of Chechnya, guided by an A-50 AWACS. In January 1996 alone the crews logged more than 1,500 hrs.

On 5 April 1991, the Roosskiye Vityazi (Russian Knights) aerobatic team was established at the Display Center at Kubinka airbase west of Moscow. This outfit is run by the 234th *Proskoorovskiy* GvIAP (*gvardeyskiy istrebeetel'nyy aviapolk* – Guards fighter regiment), and the team is the unit's 1 Sqn. Originally the team had six Flankers flown by the unit's best pilots most skilled in flying the type. The aircraft wear an eye-catching color scheme in Russia's national colors of red, white, and blue.

The Roosskiye Vityazi have mastered a wide range of formation maneuvers, including loops and barrel rolls in diamond formation, skewed loops in V formation, bomb burst, etc. One of the team's trademark stunts is a dual tail-slide: Two aircraft meet head on, as for a crossover, then go into a vertical climb and freeze simultaneously in mid-air. Airspeed during a flying display ranges from 800 to 900 km/h (444-500 kts) to just above stalling speed, and the altitude range is 60-1,500 m (197-4,921 ft.). The Roosskiye Vityazi are unique in being the world's only team to perform aerobatics with heavy fighters. The six-aircraft formation grosses at nearly 150 tons (330,687 lbs.) and has an overall wingspan in excess of 75 m (246 ft.)!

The VVS has been going through a crisis in recent years. Fuel shortages, scarce funding, and organizational difficulties are all major causes of accidents. The team's pilots only log about 100-120 flying hours each, while their Western colleagues log 500 to 600 hours annually. However,

The team's name is carried in ancient Cyrillic script above the LERXes. (Yefim Gordon)

The outer surfaces of Roosskiye Vityazi Su-27s are painted in the blue and yellow sunburst stripes of the Russian Air Force flag. (Yefim Gordon)

in some cases attrition is caused by mechanical failures.

In mid September 1997, two Su-27s (*03* and *04 Blue*), two Su-30s (*53* and *54 Blue*), and an Il-76MD support aircraft arrived at Tanagra AB near Athens to take part in a joint exercise. This was the first-ever visit to Greece by Russian military aircraft. The purpose of the visit was to participate in the Greek AF's fighter evaluation program for a McDonnell Douglas F-4E Phantom II replacement. The Flankers were up against the F-16C Block 60, Mirage 2000-5, and F-15E.

The Su-27 was never deployed to Germany. MiG-29s served there because, unlike the Flanker, they could carry tactical nuclear munitions. However, two Flanker units – the 159th GvIAP with 37 aircraft and

the 582nd IAP with 34 aircraft – were deployed to Poland. On 5 May 1992 the latter unit was disbanded and the aircraft departed for Smolensk.

According to the popular press, the IA PVO operated about 200 Su-27s in the mid '90s, with another 115 in VVS service. As of 1997, the VVS and IA PVO had some 400 Flankers on strength. Judging by press reports of the strength of the Russian armed forces, the Flanker accounts for up to 30% of Russia's fighter inventory. For the VVS and IA PVO the proportion is approximately 25% and 40%, respectively. At least 32 are in service with the Ukrainian Air Force.

The Su-27 Compared

The Su-27 has benefited from Western research; however, it does

Four Su-27Ps from the IA PVO training centre at Savostleyka AB escorting an Ilyushin/Beriyev A-50 AWACS. The latter's functions include guiding IA PVO interceptors and transmitting target data to the Su-27Ps via data link. (Yefim Gordon)

not copy any of the competitors. What does it have in common with the F-14 Tomcat, the F-15 Eagle, the F-16 Fighting Falcon, the F/A-18 Hornet, the Dassault Mirage and Rafale, the SAAB JA/AJ-37 Viggen, and JAS-39 Gripen, and what are the differences? Sure enough, it shares some design features with U.S. fighters:

- Like the F-14, it has engines in spaced nacelles and a lifting body structure (blended wing/body); unlike the Tomcat, however, the Russian fighter has tandem missile hard points between the engine nacelles;
- Like the F-15, it has horizontal attachment beams for its twin tails outboard of the engine nacelles, a large dorsal airbrake; and two-dimensional air intakes with horizontal ramps;

- Like the F-16, it has prominent LERXes and a blended wing/body design; it is statically unstable and features wingtip missile rails;
- Like the F/A-18, it has twin tails with the fins located ahead of the stabilators rather than in line with them.

The Flanker's AL-31F turbofans give it a good combat thrust-to-weight ratio determining maneuverability, acceleration and speed in a dogfight. This ratio depends on how advanced the engine is and how airframe and armament weight can be saved.

The Su-27's relative fuselage cross-section is 40% less than on third-generation fighters and 20-25% less than on the F-15C, F-16A, and F/A-18. The Su-27's fuselage is made up of several blended geometrical bodies – wing

center-section, engine nacelles, main gear fairings, and fuselage spine.

The engine nacelles are area-ruled so that their cross-section is smallest at the aircraft's overall maximum cross-section. The dorsal accessory gearboxes driven by extension shafts allow the bulky accessories to be stowed behind the wing rear spar rather than beneath the engine. The unconventional main gear design has a skewed retraction hinge axis and external downlock, and the main gear fairings have been minimized.

The Su-27 has the largest relative internal fuel volume among fourth-generation fighters. It is half as much again as that of the F-15C, which gives the Su-27 a range at sea level (S/L) equal to or better than that of modern fighters using drop tanks.

The Su-27 also has the highest structural density among fourth-generation heavy fighters, exceeding that of the F-14A and F-15C. The large-scale use of high-strength titanium resulted not only in a substantial weight saving, but also in a high-quality surface finish, improving the aerodynamics.

Western media have kept quiet about the Flanker winning in mock combat against the F-15C/D, witnessed by USAF specialists. Accompanied by an Il-76MD support aircraft, two operational Su-27UBs piloted by Maj. Gen. N. Chaga, Col. A. Kharchevskiy, and Maj. Ye. Karabasov of the VVS Combat and Conversion Training Center in Lipetsk paid a visit to Langley AFB, VA, home of the 1st TFW.

After a warm welcome and a short rest, Maj. Karabasov proposed holding a session of mock combat with an F-15 over the base so that spectators could watch. However, USAF officials deemed such a show to be "too militaristic" and offered to hold the session in a military training area 200 km (125 mi.) off the coast of Virginia instead. One can hardly blame them for not wanting to lose face in front of an audience if the Eagle lost to a visiting Flanker on its home ground.

The plan was that first a two-seat F-15D would try to shake a pursuing Su-27 off its tail, then the two would change places. Maj. Karabasov flew the Su-27UB, with a USAF pilot in the instructor's seat. A single-seat F-15C flew as chase plane. As the go signal was given the F-15D engaged full afterburner and tried to get away, but the Su-27 stayed on his tail, using full military power or minimum reheat. The Flanker's AOA never exceeded 18°.

When it was the Eagle's turn to attack, Karabasov kicked in full afterburner and entered a steep climbing turn. The F-15D followed

Two Su-27s on a training sortie. Note how the naval camouflage pattern is totally unsuitable to overland operations. (Sergey Skrynnikov)

WARBIRDTECH
SERIES

The Su-27s operated by Lipetsk training center wear the Russian flag on the fuselage or fins. (Yefim Gordon)

An early production Su-27. Dielectric fairings (the radome, starboard fin leading edge, and fin tips) were usually painted bottle-green. (Yefim Gordon Archive)

suit but couldn't keep up. After a 540° turn the Russian got an F-15 in his sights – the wrong F-15, as it turned out – he had inadvertently "shot down" the F-15C chase plane flying further aft! Realizing his mistake, Karabasov made for the other Eagle and soon got another lock-on. Try as he would, the F-15 pilot could not shake the pursuer. This proved that the Su-27's advantage in maneuverability was due to a more efficient aerodynamic layout, not just a larger lifting area.

An important feature of the Su-27 is the sculpted upper surface of the wing center section, giving the aircraft its characteristic serpentine look. Such a wing section provides a maximum lift/drag ratio during vigorous maneuvering in a dogfight – half as much again as that of a flat wing. The gain applies to a fairly broad AOA range.

The potential of the strike version was demonstrated at Dubai '93 where Arab pilots, who had taken a short training course on the Russian jet, flew the Su-30MK. In six sessions of mock combat with UAEAF Mirage 2000s (also flown by Arab pilots) the Su-30MK won four sessions, losing two; the score would have been even better if flown by Russian pilots.

As compared to other Russian fighters, the Su-27 can carry 10 AAMs whereas the MiG-29 is armed with only six (two medium-range and four short-range AAMs) and the MiG-31 can carry six or eight AAMs, including four long-range missiles. With a G limit of 9, the Su-27 is way ahead of the heavy MiG-31 in terms of maneuverability. Also, the Flanker has a range of 4,000 km (2,222 nm) on internal fuel, more than 1.5 times better than that of the Fox-hound and 2.6 times better than that of the Fulcrum. The F-15C, the best production U.S. fighter, can only match this performance with three drop-tanks and no weapons load.

THE SU-27 UNDER THE MICROSCOPE

The Su-27's cockpit canopy. Note the canopy-mounted rear view mirrors and the vulnerable pitot tube, a tempting hand grip on climbing aboard. (Sukhoi OKB archive)

The Su-27K's canards, hinged at a single pivot. The boundary splitter plate formed between the air intake and fuselage underside is readily apparent. (Yefim Gordon)

The Su-27 is a twin-engine jet fighter of blended wing/body design. The trapezoidal wings of moderate aspect ratio have large leading-edge root extensions (LERXes) allowing the fuselage to act as a lifting body. The two afterburning turbofans are located in spaced ventral nacelles to reduce interference while leaving the fuselage centerline free for two weapons pylons in tandem.

The Su-27 utilizes the electronic stability concept and has FBW controls in the pitch control circuit.

Fuselage

The fuselage is made up of five subassemblies: forward, center, and rear fuselage, and two engine nacelles.

The forward fuselage includes the fuselage nose and radome, the pressurized cockpit and canopy, and three avionics bays beside and below the cockpit with a fourth well aft of the cockpit. It also incorporates the LERXes. It is made of all-metal stressed-skin semi-monocoque structure with frames, stringers, and longitudinal beams. The nose accommodates the radar with a movable flat-plate antenna, associated drive unit, and infrared search and track (IRST) unit. The ogival radome with its metal attachment skirt is attached to a sloping fuselage mainframe and hinges upwards for access.

The pressurized cockpit is equipped with an ejection seat, engine, and flight controls. The large teardrop canopy affords the pilot an excellent all-round field of view. Downward visibility over the slightly downward-angled nose is 14°. The canopy has a fixed windshield and jettisonable aft-hinging rear section. The IRST sensor ball is mounted centrally in front of the windshield and backup pitot heads are on the cockpit sides.

Most of the avionics are installed in the aft avionics bay. The standard-

ized avionics modules are mounted on racks equipped with vibration dampers/shock absorbers. The aft avionics bay doubles as the nose wheel well. The LERXes are attached to the outer walls.

The center fuselage is divided into several bays: The load-bearing wing center-section, the forward fuel tank, and the fuselage spine front bays.

The wing center-section is an integral fuel tank with three bulkheads and ribs. The end ribs incorporate fittings for the outer wing. The underside of the wing center-section holds the main gear units, engines, and weapons hard points. It is built in two halves. The upper is riveted from aluminum alloy sheet and profiles while the lower is welded from titanium alloy sheet and profiles.

The forward integral fuel tank is located between the wing center-section and the forward fuselage. It consists of upper and lower skin panels, sidewalls and end walls, and frames.

The Su-27K's leading-edge flap. Note the fine tolerances between the deployed flap, undercarriage door, and wing hinge, as well as the close proximity of the inboard missile pylon (Yefim Gordon)

One of the main wheel wells showing the complex profile of the gear door and the neat stowage of the extremely strong main gear. The engine weapon station shows the tight ground clearance for fuselage stores. (Sukhoi OKB archive)

The Su-27's fins have dielectric tips incorporating aerials. The IFF (identification friend or foe) aerials are predictably similar to those on the MiG-29. The scrubbing on the tactical code shows how these change as operational aircraft are moved between squadrons. (Yefim Gordon Archive)

The lower skin incorporates the air intakes and weapons hardpoints while the upper skin holds for the airbrake and actuator.

The fuselage spine is a load-bearing structure housing systems and equipment. It is made up of a central section and two lateral sections. The airbrake occupies the fuselage spine above the forward integral tank. The airbrake has an area of 2.6 m² (28 sq. ft.) and a maximum deflection angle of 54°.

The aft fuselage comprises two engine nacelles, the tail unit attachment beams, and the tail cone (stinger). The engine nacelles are semi-monocoque stressed-skin structures with stringers and frames. Each nacelle consists of two sections – the center section and the engine bay proper. The nacelle center sections under the wing center section house the inlet ducts. Their mainframes carry the main gear downlocks, while the undersurfaces incorporate weapons hard points. The engines are

The air intakes – note the hardened reinforcing strips on the lower leading edges for FOD protection. The centerline stores station is also visible. (Sukhoi OKB archive)

The LERX not only adds to lift and improves airflow but also provides essential space for avionics on the port side and the 30-mm gun to starboard. (Sukhoi OKB archive)

installed so that the engine-driven accessories face upwards. Separate accessory drive gearboxes linked to the engine-mounted gearboxes by extension shafts are located aft of the rear wing spar.

The tail unit attachment beams are adjacent to the outer sides of the engine nacelles; structurally they are a continuation of the main gear fairings. The rear portions of the beams carry the fins, the stabilator hinges, and actuators. The non-load-bearing forward portions of the beams double as equipment bays.

The tail stinger incorporates the central equipment bay, the aft integral fuel tank, the tail cone (with brake parachute), and lateral aerodynamic surfaces known as flippers. The tip of the tail cone hinges up before the 'chutes pop out. The central equipment bay houses engine systems and transit pipelines. Improvements in the course of production include a lengthened and widened stinger from batch 18 onwards to accommodate chaff and flare dispensers.

Wings

The wings are cantilever mid-wing monoplane of blended

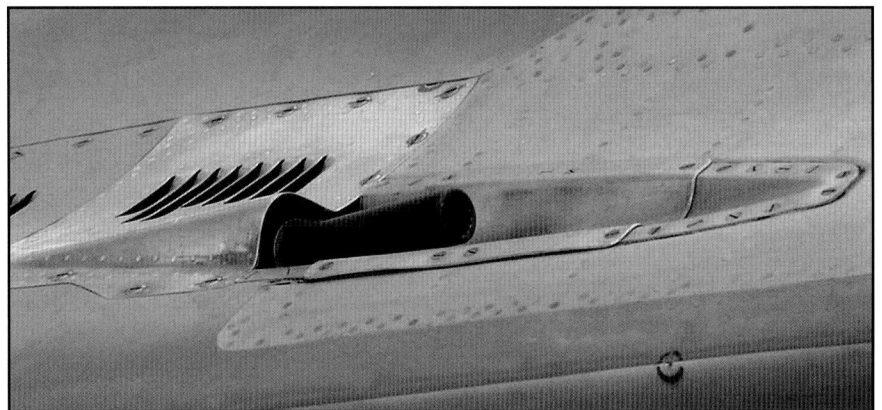

The muzzle of the GSh-301 30 mm gun in the starboard LERX. Note the heat-resistant panel for hot gas protection and the cooling louvers on the starboard side. (Yefim Gordon)

The nosewheel leg with landing/taxi lights. Note the slush guard and the hinged linking strut attached to the fuselage underside rather than fixed to the gear leg. The snug stowage beneath the cockpit can be readily visualized from this angle. (Yefim Gordon Archive)

WARBIRD**TECH**
S E R I E S

Su-27P Specifications

Engines	Landing speed
2 Lyul'ka AL-31F afterburning	225-240 km/h (125-133.3 kts)
turbofans	Rate of climb
Rating	285-300 m/sec (935-984 ft./sec)
7,600 kgp (16,755 lb st) dry	Maximum Mach number
12,500 kgp (27,557 lb st) reheat	2.35
Length, less pitot boom	Service ceiling
21.935 m (71 ft. 11.58 in.)	18,500 m (60,695 ft.)
Height on ground	Minimum turning radius
5.932 m (19 ft. 5.54 in.)	450 m (1,476 ft.)
Wingspan clean	Ferry range:
14.698 m (48 ft. 2.66 in.)	at S/L 1,400 km (777.7 nm)
with R-73 AAMs on wingtip rails	at 11,000 m (36,089 ft.)
14.948 m (49 ft. 0.50 in.)	3,880 km (2,155.5 nm)
Wing area	Combat radius
62.037 m² (667.06 sq. ft.),	at S/L 440 km (244 nm)
Takeoff weight normal	at altitude 1,380 km (766 nm)
22,500 kg (49,603 lbs.)	Endurance
overload 30,000 kg (66,137 lbs.)	4 hours
Empty operating weight	Target detection range
16,000-16,300 kg	at S/L 80-100 km (44-55 nm)
(35,273-35,934 lbs.)	at altitude 30- 40 km (16-22 nm)
Maximum ordnance load	Kill altitude
6,000 kg (13,227 lbs.)	20-27,000 m
Internal fuel load:	Target speed (kill possible)
normal 5,270 kg (11,618 lbs.)	incoming 210-3,100 km/h
maximum 9,400-9,850	(116-1,722 kts)
kg (20,723-21,715 lbs.)	outbound 210-2,400 km/h
Thrust-to-weight ratio	(116-1,333 kts)
1.2	Take off run in full afterburner
Top speed at sea level	650-700 m (2,132-2,296 ft.)
1,380 km/h (766.6 kts)	Landing run with brake
at altitude 2,500 km/h	parachute 620-700 m
(1,388.8 kts)	(2,034-2,296 ft.)
Minimum speed	G limit
200 km/h (111 kts)	+9

wing/body design, built in three sections (integral center section and two outer wings). Leading edge sweep 42°, thickness-to-chord ratio 3-5%, span 14.7 m (48 ft. 2.74 in.), area 62.04 m² (667.1 sq. ft.), aspect ratio 3.5, taper 3.4.

The wings have two-section LE flaps with an area of 4.6 m² (49.46 sq. ft.) and flaperons of 4.9 m² (52.68 sq. ft.). The flaperons can be deflected +35°/-20°. The LE flaps and flaperons can be lowered during maneuvers at up to 860 km/h (477 kts) IAS.

The outer wings are three-spar structures with integral fuel tanks. Each wing has reinforced ribs acting as weapons hard points, including one at the tip. The center section accommodates the main gear units. The port LE root extension (LERX) houses avionics while the starboard houses the 30-mm single-barrel gun and incorporates cooling louvres. A heat-resistant steel panel is fitted ahead of the gun muzzle.

Each outer wing consists of a torsion box, front and rear parts, LE flaps, flaperons, and a wingtip fairing. The torsion box is made up of three spars, multi-segment upper and lower skins, and ribs. The front part houses pipe and cable runs and LE flap actuators; similarly, the rear part houses pipe and cable runs and flaperon actuators.

Tail Unit

The Su-27 has differentially movable trapezoidal stabilizers for pitch and roll control (stabilators). These have a leading-edge sweep of 45°; stabilator span is 9.8 m (32 ft. 1.82 in.), and an area of 12.2 m² (131.18 sq. ft.). For pitch control the stabilators are deflected +20° through -15°; for roll control they are deflected 10°.

The twin trapezoidal fins, mounted on the tail unit attachment beams, have a two-spar structure with a main rib at the root. Multiple hydraulic actuators within the fins actuate the rudders that have an area of 1.75 m² (18.8 sq. ft.) each and can be deflected by 25°. Total vertical tail area is 15.4 m² (165.59 sq. ft.), leading-edge sweep is 40°. The fin tips and the starboard fin LE are formed by dielectric fairings over navigation and communications aerials. To improve directional stability and spinning characteristics, two ventral fins with an area of 1.25 m² (13.44 sq. ft.) are fitted to the tail unit.

Landing Gear

Landing gear is the hydraulically retractable tricycle type, with a single wheel on each unit; all units retract forward. Unusually, the downlocks of the telescopic main units are

The Su-27's rugged main gear with a single strut looks simple until the smooth conformal profile achieved after retraction is appreciated. (Yefim Gordon Archive)

An R-27R radar-homing anti-aircraft missile on the centerline station between the intakes. In the foreground is the nose gear support strut. (Yefim Gordon)

R-27R radar-homing AAMs on the intake-mounted pylons and centerline pylons. These pylons require stores to be ejected downward before the motors fire to maintain separation from the aircraft underbelly. (Yefim Gordon)

mounted directly on the engine nacelles, removing the need for breaker struts, and they are enclosed by prominent fairings.

The semi-levered suspension nose unit is located fairly close to the aircraft's center of gravity, giving the Su-27 a remarkably small turning radius on the ground. It is fitted with a KN-27 non-braking wheel with a 680-260 mm (26.7-10.2 in.) tire and mud/snow/slush guard for foreign object damage (FOD) protection. The nose wheel well is closed by a single large door opening to starboard. Landing gear wheelbase and track are 5.8 m (19 ft.) and 4.34 m (14 ft. 2.8 in.), respectively.

Engines

Engines are two Lyul'ka (NPO "Saturn") AL-31F afterburning turbofans rated at 7,600 kgp (16,755 lb st) dry and 12,500 kgp (27,557 lb st) reheat. The engines have two-dimensional supersonic inlets with horizontal ramps.

The AL-31F is a two-shaft turbofan with a four-stage adjustable low-pressure (LP) compressor, a nine-stage high-pressure (HP) compressor (the first stages of which are likewise adjustable), an annular combustion chamber, a single-stage air-cooled HP turbine, a single-stage air-cooled LP turbine, an afterburner, and a convergent-divergent axi-symmetric supersonic nozzle. Bypass ratio (BPR) is about 0.59. Core and bypass flows are mixed aft of the turbine. The engine has a closed-circuit lubrica-

The IRST fairing houses the optoeletronic sighting system that can link to a helmet-mounted sight. The primitive fixing method is surprising given the smooth profiling of the basic airframe. The engineer apparently still dominates the aerodynamicist. (Sukhoi OKB archive)

The Su-27K's nosewheel leg with landing/taxi lights. Note the smaller but equally effective slush guard and the horizontal bar for tow-bar attachment. (Yefim Gordon)

The N-001 (RLPK-27) fire-control radar seen with the radome opened for maintenance. This 80- to 100-km range radar can track 10 targets and allows the WCS to engage two targets simultaneously. (Sukhoi OKB archive)

tion system and a self-contained turbostarter (APU) connected to the accessories gearbox.

To improve handling, the nozzles are inclined 5° down to ensure that the thrust line passes through the aircraft's CG. The nozzle features a number of inner petals hinged to the aft end of the afterburner chamber and controlled by hydraulic rams. They form a critical section in all engine-operating modes. Supersonic petals forming the divergent part of the nozzle are hinged to them. A third set of flexible petals forms the outer contour. Their sprung front ends are inserted under the nacelle skin, ensuring a smooth transition from nacelle to nozzle at all times. Their aft ends are attached to the inner petals by flexible links so that an annular gap remains. Engine bay cooling air is bled through this gap.

The adjustable supersonic air intakes have a rectangular section at the inlets and horizontal control ramps. To prevent boundary layer ingestion, the intakes are set at a distance from the wing undersurface so that the intake upper lip acts as a boundary layer splitter plate. A v-shaped fairing spilling the boundary layer connects the intake lip to the

The Flanker Family Compared

	Su-27P	Su-27UB
Crew	1	2
Engines	AL-31F	AL-31F
Rating per engine in full afterburner	12,500 kgp (27,557 lb st)	12,500 kgp (27,557 lb st)
Length	21.935 m (71 ft. 11.6 in.)	21.935 m (71 ft. 11.6 in.)
Height on ground	5.932 m (19 ft. 5.54 in.)	6.357 m (20 ft. 10.27 in.)
Wing span	14.698 m (48 ft. 2.66 in.)	14.698 m (48 ft. 2.66 in.)
Wing area	62.0 m² (666 sq. ft.)	62.0 m² (666 sq. ft.)
Operating empty weight	16,000-16,300 kg (35,273-35,934 lbs.)	17,500 kg (38,580 lbs.)
Normal TOW	22,500 kg (49,603 lbs.)	24,000 kg (52,910 lbs.)
MTOW	30,000 kg (66,137 lbs.)	30,500 kg (67,239 lbs.)
Internal fuel load	9,400 kg (20,723 lbs.)	9,400 kg (20,723 lbs.)
Ordnance load	6,000 kg (13,227 lbs.)	n/a
Top speed:		
at S/L	1,380 km/h (766 kts)	n/a
at 11,000 m (36,089 ft.)		2,125 km/h (1,180 kts)
Unstick speed	n/a	n/a
Landing speed	225-240 km/h (125-133 kts)	235-250 km/h (130-138 kts)
Max. Mach no.	2.35	2.0
Service ceiling	18,500 m (60,695 ft.)	17,250 m (56,594 ft.)
G limit	9	9
Range w. max fuel:		
at S/L	1,400 km (777 nm)	1,300 km (722 nm)
at high altitude	3,900 km (2,166 nm)	3,000 km (1,666 nm)
w/one top-up	—	—
w/two top-ups	—	—
Takeoff run	650-700 m (2,132-2,296 ft.)	750-800 m (2,460-2,624 ft.)
Landing run	620-700 m (2,034-2,296 ft.)	650-700 m (2,132-2,296 ft.)
Armament:		
Gun	GSh-301 30 mm	GSh-301 30 mm
Hard points	10	10

wing. Its shape is optimized for minimum drag. The three-segment intake ramps and auxiliary blow-in intake grilles obviate the need for bleed doors. An ARV-40A digital control unit controls intake ramp position.

A movable FOD protection grille is fitted at the diffuser. Its aft end is hinged to the lower surface of the inlet duct so that any foreign objects retained by the grille are trapped during retraction, which is simultaneous with landing gear retraction.

Fuel system

The Su-27's fuel system comprises four integral fuel tanks – three in the fuselage and one in the wings – fuel transfer and delivery pumps, and fuel metering equipment. Total internal fuel volume is approximately 12,000 lit (2,640 Imp. gal.). The fuel load is 9,400 kg (20,723 lbs.) at a specific fuel gravity of 0.785 g/cm³. The fuel system is identical for single-seat and two-seat versions.

Armament

Built-in armament consists of a single GSh-301 30-mm quick-firing single-barrel gun designed by V. P. Gryazev and A. G. Shipunov. The gun has an ammo supply of 150 rounds and rate of fire is 1,500 rpm.

WARBIRDTECH
SERIES

Su-27SK	Su-27SMK	Su-30
1	1	2
AL-31F	AL-31F	AL-31F
12,500 kgp (27,557 lb st)	12,500 kgp (227,557 lb st)	12,500 kgp (27,557 lb st)
21.935 m (71 ft. 11.6 in.)	21.935 m (71 ft. 11.6 in.)	21.935 m (71 ft. 11.6 in.)
5.932 m (19 ft. 5.54 in.)	5.932 m (19 ft. 5.54 in.)	6.357 m (20 ft. 10.27 in.)
14.698 m (48 ft. 2.66 in.)	14.698 m (48 ft. 2.66 in.)	14.698 m (48 ft. 2.66 in.)
62.0 m² (666 sq. ft.)	62.0 m² (666 sq. ft.)	62.0 m² (666 sq. ft.)
n/a	n/a	n/a
n/a	23,700 kg (52,248 lbs.)	24,800 kg (54,673 lbs.)
33,000 kg (72,751 lbs.)	33,000 kg (72,751 lbs.)	30,450 kg (67,129 lbs.)
9,400 kg (20,723 lbs.)	9,400 kg (20,723 lbs.)	9,400 kg (20,723 lbs.)
8,000 kg (17,636 lbs.)	8,000 kg (17,636 lbs.)	8,000 kg (17,636 lbs.)
1,380 km/h (766 kts)	1,380 km/h (766 kts)	1,380 km/h (766 kts)
2,500 km/h (1,388 kts)	2,500 km/h (1,388 kts)	2,500 km/h (1,388 kts)
n/a	n/a	n/a
225-240 km/h (125-133 kts)	225-240 km/h (125-133 kts)	n/a
2.35	2.35	2.35
18,500 m (60,695 ft.)	18,000 m (59,055 ft.)	18,000 m (59,055 ft.)
9	9	9
1,560 km (866 nm)	n/a	n/a
3,680 km (2,044 nm)	3,790/4,390 km (2,105/2,438 nm)	3,000 km (1,666 nm)
—	5,200 km (2,888 nm)	5,200 km (2,888 nm)
—	n/a	6,990 km (3,883 nm)
700-800 m (2,296-2,624 ft.)	650 m (2,132 ft.)	550 m (1,804 ft.)
620 m (2,034 ft.)	620 m (2,034 ft.)	670 m (2,198 ft.)
GSh-301 30 mm	GSh-301 30 mm	GSh-301 30 mm
10	12	10

The Su-27 can carry missiles and bombs on 10 hard points: three under each outer wing, one under each engine nacelle, and two in tandem on the centerline. Multiple ejector racks (MERs) can be fitted to the fuselage and innermost wing hard points.

Avionics and Equipment

The Su-27 has a complete avionics suite permitting operation in VFR and IFR conditions throughout the altitude envelope. This is divided into five main groups: the SUV-27 weapons targeting complex (*sistema oopravleniya vo'orouzheniyem* – armament control system), the flight and navigational instruments, the communications suite, the defensive avionics suite, and the flight data recorders (black boxes).

The SUV-27 targeting complex is a duplex system built around the fire control radar and the IRST. It permits the use of AAMs in beyond visual range (BVR) and dogfight conditions, ensures target acquisition and tracking by radar and IRST (in BVR conditions), visual target acquisition and tracking during a dogfight, and identification friend or foe (IFF).

The SUV-27 complex comprises:
• the RLPK-27 radar sighting system (*rahdiolokatseeonnaya preetsel'naya sistema*);

The Flanker Family Compared *continued*

	Su-30MK	Su-27K (Su-33)
Crew	1	1
Engines	Luyl'ka AL-31F	Luyl'ka AL-31F
Rating per engine in full afterburner	12,500 kgp (27,557 lb st)	12,500 kgp (27,557 lb st)
Length	21.935 m (71 ft. 11.6 in.)	21.935 m (71 ft. 11.6 in.)
Height on ground	6.357 m (20 ft. 10.27 in.)	5.932 m (19 ft. 5.54 in.)
Wing span	14.698 m (48 ft. 2.66 in.)	14.698 m (48 ft. 2.66 in.)
Wing area	62.0 m² (666 sq. ft.)	62.0 m² (666 sq. ft.)
Operating empty weight	n/a	n/a
Normal TOW	25,670 kg (56,591 lbs.)	29,940 kg (66,005 lbs.)
MTOW	34,000 kg (74,955 lbs.)	33,000 kg (72,751 lbs.)
Internal fuel load	9,400 kg (20,723 lbs.)	n/a
Ordnance load	8,000 kg (17,636 lbs.)	6,500 kg (14,329 lbs.)
Top speed:		
at S/L	1,380 km/h (766 kts)	1,200 km/h (666 kts)
	at 11,000 m (36,089 ft.)	2,500 km/h (1,388 kts)
Unstick speed	n/a	140 km/h (77 kts)
Landing speed	225-240 km/h (125-133 kts)	235-250 km/h (130-138 kts)
Max. Mach no.	2.35	2.17
Service ceiling	18,000 m (59,055 ft.)	17,000 m (55,774 ft.)
G limit	9	8
Range w. max fuel:		
at S/L	n/a	n/a
at high altitude	3,000-3,200 km (1,666-1,777 nm)	3,000 km (1,666 nm)
w/one top-up	5,200 km (2,888 nm)	n/a
w/two top-ups	6,990 km (3,883 nm)	n/a
Takeoff run	550 m (1,804 ft.)	n/a
Landing run	670 m (2,198 ft.)	n/a
Armament:		
Gun	GSh-301 30 mm	GSh-301 30 mm
Hard points	10	10

- the OEPS-27 optoelectronic sighting system (*optiko-elektronnaya preetsel'naya sistema*) comprising the IRST unit and a helmet-mounted sight (HMS);
- a common indication system;
- an IFF system;
- a command link system allowing target data to be transmitted to the aircraft by data link;
- the SUO-27 weapons control system (*sistema oopravleniya orouzhiyem*).

The RLPK-27 sighting system comprises the N-001 "Mech" (Sword) coherent pulse-Doppler fire control radar developed by NPO "Fazotron" in Moscow and the TsVM-80 computer. The radar has a scanner diameter of 1.076 m (3 ft. 6.36 in.) and a target detection range of 80 km (44 nm) in the forward hemisphere and 30-40 km (16-22 nm) in the rear hemisphere if the target's radar cross section (RCS) is about 3 m² (32.25 sq. ft.). Its functions include:

- detecting aerial targets, including those flying below the aircraft's flight level (look-down/shoot-down capability);
- designating priority threats

WARBIRDTECH
S E R I E S

Su-27M (Su-35)	Su-37	Su-34 (Su-32FN)
1	1	2
Luyl'ka AL-31FM	Luyl'ka AL-31FP	Luyl'ka AL-31FM
12,800 kgp (28,218 lb st)	12,800 kgp (28,218 lb st)	12,800 kgp (28,218 lb st)
21.935 m (71 ft. 11.6 in.)	21.935 m (71 ft. 11.6 in.)	23.3 m (76 ft. 5.32 in.)
5.932 m (19 ft. 5.54 in.)	5.932 m (19 ft. 5.54 in.)	6.0 m? (19 ft. 8.22 in.)
14.698 m (48 ft. 2.66 in.)	14.698 m (48 ft. 2.66 in.)	14.698 m (48 ft. 2.66 in.)
62.0 m² (666 sq. ft.)	62.0 m² (666 sq. ft.)	62.0 m² (666 sq. ft.)
18,400 kg (40,564 lbs.)	n/a	n/a
25,700 kg (56,657 lbs.)	n/a	42,000 kg (92,592 lbs.)
34,000 kg (74,955 lbs.)	n/a	44,360 kg (97,795 lbs.)
n/a	n/a	n/a
8,000 kg (17,636 lbs.)	8,000 kg (17,636 lbs.)	8,000 kg (17,636 lbs.)
1,380 km/h (766 kts)	1,380 km/h (766 kts)	1,380 km/h (766 kts)
2,300 km/h (1,277 kts)	2,500 km/h (1,388 kts)	2,500 km/h (1,388 kts)
n/a	n/a	n/a
225-240 km/h (125-133 kts)	225-240 km/h (125-133 kts)	n/a
2.35	2.35	1.8
18,000 m (59,055 ft.)	18,000 m (59,055 ft.)	n/a
9/10	9/10	7?
n/a	1,390 km (772 nm)	n/a
4,000 km (2,222 nm)	3,300 km (1,833 nm)	4,000 km (2,222 nm)
6,500 km (3,611 nm)	6,500 km (3,611 nm)	7,000 km (3,888 nm)
n/a	n/a	n/a
n/a	n/a	n/a
n/a	n/a	n/a
GSh-301 30 mm	GSh-301 30 mm	GSh-301 30 mm
12	12	12

among the targets it is currently tracking;

- continuously tracking the target currently under attack (in azimuth and range);
- illuminating the target for semi-active radar homing (SARH) weapons;
- tracking enemy ECM sources;
- missile-aiming in a dogfight;
- downloading commands to AAMs both before and after launch in radio-corrected guidance mode, also in an ECM environment;
- determining conditions when AAMs can be fired;
- feeding target data to the opto-electronic sighting system.

A crucial feature of the N-001 is its high ECM resistance. The radar enables the Su-27 to attack two targets simultaneously.

Control System

The Su-27 family is equipped with the SDU-27 FBW control system (*sistema distantseeonnovo oopravleniya*). It controls the statically unstable aircraft in the pitch channel, provides adequate stability and controllability

The Su-27 tail section shows the long engine nozzles and the space available for later thrust vectoring modifications within existing CG limits. The nozzles are, however, vulnerable to attack by heat-seeking missiles. (Yefim Gordon Archive)

in the roll and yaw channels, enhances maneuverability, acts as an electronic angle of attack and G limiter in order to prevent a departure, and decreases aerodynamic airframe loads.

Hydraulics

Since the Su-27 is equipped with an FBW control system incorporating powerful and fast-operating hydraulic actuators, a reliable and efficient hydraulic system is a must.

Pneumatic System

The pneumatic system is used for emergency gear extension, avionics bay pressurization, canopy operation and sealing, etc.

Environmental Control System

The Su-27 is equipped with an unusual environmental control system comprising an autonomous evaporation-type air conditioning system and a liquid-cooling system. It maintains the required temperature in the cockpit, cools the air for the pilot's pressure suit, and cools and pressurizes the

The Su-27 wing section outboard of the intakes. The lack of lift devices allows considerable strengthening within the wing for stores carriage and maneuverability. (Yefim Gordon Archive)

avionics bays. The liquid-cooling system caters exclusively for the radar set.

Crew Rescue System and Crew Gear

The Su-27 family is equipped with K-36DM Srs two zero-zero ejec-

tion seats developed by the Zvezda Design Bureau under Guy Il'yich Severin. This ejection seat has become the standard seat of all Soviet (Russian) combat aircraft since the mid-70s. The G load during ejection does not exceed 20 Gs.

FOREIGN FLANKERS

Angola

Angola had taken delivery of eight Su-27s at Catumbela with the balance of seven expected imminently. Pilots had reportedly trained in Belarus, the presumed source of the aircraft, though technical support came from Ukraine.

Belorussia

Like the Ukraine, Belorussia operates a number of Su-27s inherited from the Soviet Air Force. These aircraft retain their Soviet-style red stars but are presumed sold on to Angola.

China

Export sales began in August 1992 when the People's Republic of China (mainland China) took delivery of 20 single-seat Su-27SKs and four Su-27UBK trainers. These were soon followed by a further 24 aircraft, bringing the total to 36 single-seaters and 12 two-seaters. China also acquired manufacturing rights – with the condition that the license-built aircraft would not be exported.

Originally the Su-27s were based at Wuhan. Later, half the Flanker force moved to Liancheng AB. Disaster struck on 23 April 1997. A hurricane ripped across the flight line at Liancheng, knocking out 17 of the 24 fighters based there. Press reports stated that at least three aircraft were damaged beyond repair, adding that Russia could look forward to more Su-27 orders from China. Most aircraft were rebuilt and back in service by autumn.

After some quality control problems, 28 extra Russian-built Su-27UBKs were procured and delivered 2000-02. The first 50 aircraft were being assembled from Russian-supplied kits of diminishing completeness, and the Chinese aircraft always include at least 30 percent Komsomolsk content. The first 10 kits were stated to have been 100 percent complete, but by the year 2000 Chinese production switched to the Su-30MKK after 80 aircraft. The initial batch of 10 Su-30MKKs was delivered on 20 December 2000; nine followed in March/April 2001 and 10 more on 21 August.

Ethiopia

Ethiopia received the first of eight second-hand Flankers from Russia in late 1998.

The Ukrainian AF took possession of all the Flankers based on home soil, about 90 remained operational in 1997. Most Su-27s wear blue tactical codes and operate from flightlines rather than hardened shelters. (Chris Lofting)

PLAAF Su-27SKs being readied for flights on the Chinese mainland. The Flankers were the first Soviet arms sold to China for 30 years.

On 22 March 1998 the aircraft were used operationally for the first time. Three Su-30Ks participated in the Vayu Shakti '98 exercise in Pokhran, Rajasthan. The fighters demolished 11 targets, including a mock runway, with pinpoint bomb strikes. The Su-30 amazed the audience, which included some 25 foreign military attachés, with an aerobatics display that culminated in a mock dogfight with a MiG-29.

The final requirement may be as high as 140 with a parallel upgrade program running up to the final deliveries from HAL in 2017.

Indonesia

In late 1999, there were reports that Indonesia announced in March 2003 that two Su-27s and two Su-35s would be purchased immediately as a prelude to the acquisition of a total of 48 Flanker versions over following four years.

Kazakhstan

This republic is receiving 32 from Russia, most recently six in 1997, four in January 1999 and four during 2000 (with 12 then outstanding), as compensation for the return of Tu-95 bombers and for alleged environmental and ecological damage.

The Ukraine

After the collapse of the Soviet Union, the newly formed Ukrainian Air Force took possession of all Su-27s based in the Ukraine (66-70 aircraft). It was not long before UAF Flankers began paying courtesy visits abroad. A couple of specially-painted aircraft put in an appearance at the 1996 Royal International Air Tattoo (RIAT) at RAF Fairford.

On 10-14 June 1997, a delegation of the USAF's 4th TFW/333rd TFS

India

On 30 November 1996 Russia and India signed a contract for the delivery of 40 Su-30K multi-role fighters to the Indian Air Force.

Under the contract the fighters would be delivered in four batches within a five-year time frame and progressively upgraded from batch to batch. The first batch of eight aircraft was delivered ahead of schedule in the spring of 1997. The fighters were then reassembled and test flown by IAPO personnel. IAF pilots and ground crews took their training at Zhukovskiy between January and April 1997.

The initial eight aircraft are Su-30Ks differing from Russian AF Su-30s only slightly in navigation equipment. Starting in the year 2000, however, Su-30MKIs were delivered. These are, in effect, next-generation aircraft and much more capable than the Su-30K. The Su-30MKI features canards and thrust-vectoring AL-31FP engines for enhanced maneuverability, as well as a completely new avionics suite. The Su-30Ks were later updated to this standard. The contract also provides for possible integration of Western avionics. India has contributed to the design of the Su-30MKI's avionics suite, the first batch of which has been delivered.

WARBIRDTECH
S E R I E S

A photo of Kazakhstan Air Force Su-27, one of a small batch donated in 1996. Note the under-wing rocket pods. (Vyacheslav Martynyuk)

from Seymour Johnson AFB, North Carolina, paid a friendly visit to the UAF base in Mirgorod on a "brother base" mission. The guests arrived in four F-15E Strike Eagles. The highlight of the event was the flying display given by both guests and hosts.

United States

On 26 November 1995, the first of two Su-27s was reported as delivered to the USA inside an An-124 for an unknown purpose, believed to be support of military training exercises.

Uzbekistan

30 Flankers have been reported.

Vietnam

Vietnam was the second foreign operator. The Vietnamese People's Air Force (VPAF) order was much smaller – five Su-27SKs and a single Su-27UBK worth U.S. $180 million. The aircraft were delivered in 1995-96 and Vietnamese Flanker pilots took their training in Russia. In late January 1997 Vietnam signed a U.S. $180 million order for six more aircraft. Possible deliveries of 24 more Flankers over the next four years are being discussed; the deal is worth an estimated U.S. $800 million.

On 6 December 1997 a Russian Air Force An-124 carrying two Su-27UBs destined for the Vietnamese Air Force crashed on the outskirts of Irkutsk. The airlifter and its cargo were destroyed. Russia replaced the fighters. There are indications that future deliveries may be Su-30s rather than regular Flanker-Cs. An upgrade is expected, since Vietnam requires aircraft to use R-77 AAMs, ICh-29, Kh-31, and ICh-59 ASMs.

A number of nations are still negotiating for Flankers, however, no firm orders or deliveries are confirmed. These include:

Japan

Japan has been reported to be interested in two aircraft for evaluation/aggressor use, but Sukhoi is unwilling to sell fewer than six. Two Japanese pilots underwent a U.S. $300,000 46-day training program on the Su-27 in early 1998.

Malaysia

Malaysia was reportedly considering an Su-27 purchase. On 22 January 2001 the *Utusan Malaysia* daily reported the final stages of a deal for the delivery of Su-30MKM fighters. A U.S. $900 million contract was initialled 19 May 2003. Financial constraints due to the 2004 tsunami may compromise the order.

Syria

Syria has requested 14 Flankers. Some unconfirmed reports suggest 17 in service, but others state that only four were in service by mid-2000 – two at Minkah AB and two at Damascus.

Yemen

This People's Republic is negotiating for "one squadron" of Flankers.

To Conclude

The Sukhoi OKB's evolutionary approach to the basic Flanker design has led to the appearance of a whole family of combat aircraft developed for various roles. The existing spin-offs of the Su-27 can replace at least 10 assorted second- and third-generation types now in service with the Russian Air Force. The high degree of airframe, engine, and avionics commonality between the members of the Flanker family facilitates production, operation, and conversion training. The latest versions provide Russia, India, and China with arguably the world's most advanced tactical fighter.

However, considering Russia's current economic situation, these promising aircraft are facing an uncertain future. Defense budget cuts and lack of funding for R&D have caused development and tests of new aircraft to drag on for years and years while some advanced projects have been shelved altogether.

SUKHOI SU-27 SCALE MODEL KITS

BY RICHARD MARMO

Those of you who have read the MiG-29 Scale Model Kit Appendix already know this, but I'll restate it for new readers. In a nutshell, today's modelers have a wide choice of accurate and highly detailed Soviet/Russian aircraft subjects. This is a stark contrast to 50 years ago when you were pretty much limited to MiG-15s from Airfix and that ficticious MiG-19 from Aurora. All of which brings us to this book's subject, the Sukhoi Su-27. Who would've ever dreamed that we would have even a single kit of the Su-27 in any scale, never mind a dozen or so? Let's take a look at what you have to pick from.

First up is the kit that must be considered the gold standard when it comes to Su-27 kits – an Su-27B Flanker in 1/32 scale from Trumpeter. Pricey at $149.95, one look inside the box and the tab becomes reasonable indeed. This little beauty is a true jewel.

Trumpeter's magnificent 1/32-scale Su-27 box. As large as the box is (23-1/2"), the finished model is even larger (over 28" long and 19" wingspan).

The large 16" x 23-1/2" x 5" box contains the parts for an even larger model, and the packaging blows you away before you ever get to the parts. Upper and lower fuselage halves each have their own card-

stock sleeves. If that's not enough, each half is held down with twist ties over foam padding. It also features a couple of slipcover boxes inside the box. One holds foam-padded air intakes and the nose cone. The second box? That one contains the foam-wrapped canopy and windscreen, a sprue of other clear parts, photoetch fret (nickel, not brass), the six-part tailpipes, film instrument panel, parts for optional metal landing gear, screws, and three hollow rubber tires (rubber, not vinyl) that are complete with accurate tread patterns.

All the other parts are contained on eight sprues and packed in four bags. Instructions take the form of a 24-page manual. A large, color three-view takes care of the markings and camouflage and the large decal sheet gets its own bag.

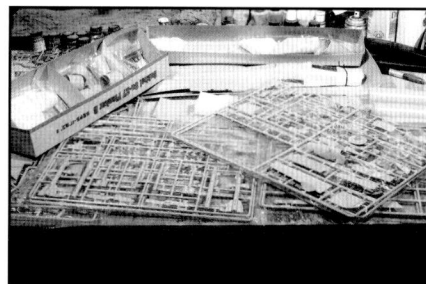

Parts, parts, and more parts. The boxtop says 350, but if you count every screw and photoetch hinge, it's over 400. Also, in this shot you can see the slipcover boxes that protect the air intakes, canopy and other components.

Every control surface is movable, along with the air brake and the landing gear oleos, which are spring loaded so that they actually work. Total number of parts? Three hundred fifty. If you're partial to 1/32 scale and have a fondness for Soviet/Russian aircraft, this one's an absolute must.

There's way too much in the box to show it in a single photo. Here you can see the instructions, color guide, decals, and the protective sleeve for the fuselage halves. In the foreground is one of the fuselage halves fastened to its cardstock carrier with foam padding and twist ties.

Prefer your Flanker in 1/48 scale? Academy has three different versions in their line and Hobbycraft Canada offers one as well. I haven't seen any of these, so I can't comment intelligently on them. Do keep in mind that Eduard produces aftermarket cockpit detail sets for the Su-27 in both 1/32 and 1/48.

If you're still cramped for display space or you've spent years developing a comprehensive aviation collection in 1/72 scale, there's no need to despair. Airfix, Berkut, Hasegawa, Italeri, and Revell all produce kits of the Su-27B in that scale. The Italeri Su-27B is not currently available, leaving the "Su-27D" as their effort. That's the navalized version with canard wings mounted forward of the main wing and an arrestor hook under the aft fuselage.

As it turns out, the Italeri offering is literally the only game in town (at the time this is written) if you want to add a Flanker-D (or Sea Flanker) to your collection… in any scale. Well, there is one other Flanker-D, but that falls into a special category. At any rate, the Italeri kit is quite nice in its own right with their typically delicate recessed surface detail. Of course, if you're planning a contest entry, you need to spend some time in the cockpit.

That special case I was talking about? Trumpeter produces a 1/350-scale kit of the aircraft carrier Kuznetsov, complete with a batch of 1/350-scale Flanker-D aircraft to spot on the flight deck. They also offer a separate box of Su-27D Flankers (six to a box), presumably so that you can have a larger complement of Sea Flankers on your carrier.

But if you happen to like your models really small, there's certainly nothing wrong with buying a box

Giving new meaning to the phrase "I'm gonna run out to pick up a six-pack" is this six-pack of 1/350-scale Su-27Ds from Trumpeter.

and building up your own squadron of Su-27Ds. And if you're wondering what a 1/350 Su-27D looks like, check out the photograph below. Comprised of 14 parts including a clear canopy and the option to build it with the wings folded, this little fella's cuter'n a speckled pup. Or it would be if you took the extra time to paint and decal it. And yes, decals are included. I just threw one together, without bothering to paint it or even clean up the seams, so you could see an assembled model. Of course, "throw" may not be the right word considering that most of the parts are so small that it takes an OptiVisor to see them and a pair of precision tweezers to handle them!

Whatever scale you prefer, from the humongous to the miniscule, if you've been wanting to add an Su-27 to your collection, the kits are available. Take your pick.

For lovers of the truly miniscule, this little Su-27D has to take the prize. The tricycle landing gear actually fits on a good ol' American two-bit piece (that's a quarter for the uninitiated). Note that I've built this model with one wing folded to show the option provided. And don't forget the OptiVisor and tweezers when you tackle this one. You'll need 'em.

Italeri's Su-27D Sea Flanker (or Flanker D) is offered in 1/72 scale. This is a very nice kit in its own right and your only choice if you want to build an Su-27D.

ENDNOTES

1. Later changed to "lightweight tactical fighter" (LTF).

2. Institoot teoreteecheskoy i prikladnoy mekhahniki – Institute of Theoretical and Applied Mechanics, Siberian division of the USSR Academy of Sciences.

3. Lyul'ka had pioneered the idea back in the '50s but was not in a position to proceed with it; it was Solovyov who built the world's first turbofan, the D-20P which powered the Tu-124 Cookpot airliner.

4. K stands for kompleks [vo'orouzheniya] – armament system.

5. Unlike Western military aircraft (which have serial numbers allowing positive identification), Soviet military aircraft have two-digit tactical codes that are usually simply the number of the aircraft in its unit. Three-digit codes are rare and are usually allocated to development aircraft only, often tying in with the construction number (c/n), i.e., manufacturer's serial number.

6. An official grade reflecting pilot expertise and experience.

7. Aviatsiya voyenno-morskovo flota – Naval Aviation.

8. The T10-7 and T10-8 were radically different aircraft and are described separately.

9. Su-27s (Su-27Ps) have construction numbers (c/ns) commencing with 369110. The first four digits are probably codes for the factory and the sub-type. 10 denotes the aircraft type (T-10); these two digits are present in the c/ns of other Flanker versions built both by KnaAPO and elsewhere. The remaining five digits are individual; e.g., 05705 = Batch 5, assembled by team 7, 5th aircraft in batch. Thus, c/n 36911005705 corresponds to fuselage line number (f/n) 0505 (Batch 5, 5th aircraft in batch).

10. LMK = lyotno-modeleeruyuschchiy kompleks – "flight modelling complex" or total in-flight simulator (TIFS).

11. Irkootskoye aviatseeonnoye proizvodstvennoye obyedineniye – Irkutsk aircraft production association.

12. This is a common Soviet (Russian) Air Force slang term for conversion trainer derivatives of fighters and translates loosely as "Two-Sticks," being derived from spahrennoye oopravleniye – dual controls. (Double Trouble would be more fitting, perhaps?).

13. UPAZ = oonifitseerovannyy podvesnoy agregaht zapravki – standardized suspended (i.e., external) refueling unit; in other words, a podded hose drum unit (HDU) like those found on, e.g., the VC-10 K. Mk 1/Mk 2. The "standardized" part of the name means that it can be used by various types – the Il-78/78M, Su-24M, etc.

14. Istrebeetel'nyy aviapolk – fighter regiment = fighter wing.